3

PANORAMA

BUILDING PERSPECTIVE THROUGH LISTENING

DAPHNE MACKEY

LAURIE BLASS

CHERRY CAMPBELL

with KATHRYN HEINZE and HELEN HUNTLEY

OXFORD

UNIVERSITY PRESS

OXFORD
UNIVERSITY PRESS

198 Madison Avenue
New York, NY 10016 USA

Great Clarendon Street, Oxford OX2 6DP UK

Oxford University Press is a department of the University of Oxford.
It furthers the University's objective of excellence in research, scholarship,
and education by publishing worldwide in

Oxford New York

Auckland Cape Town Dar es Salaam Hong Kong Karachi
Kuala Lumpur Madrid Melbourne Mexico City Nairobi
New Delhi Shanghai Taipei Toronto

With offices in

Argentina Austria Brazil Chile Czech Republic France Greece
Guatemala Hungary Italy Japan Poland Portugal Singapore
South Korea Switzerland Thailand Turkey Ukraine Vietnam

OXFORD and OXFORD ENGLISH are registered trademarks of
Oxford University Press.

© Oxford University Press 2007

Database right Oxford University Press (maker)

Developer: Angela M. Castro, English Language Trainers
Editorial Director: Sally Yagan
Publishing Manager: Pietro Alongi
Editor: Rob Freire
Associate Editor: Beverley Langevine
Art Director: Robert Carangelo
Senior Designer: Michael Steinhofer
Art Editor: Robin Fadool
Production Manager: Shanta Persaud
Production Controller: Soniya Kulkarni

STUDENT BOOK ISBN: 978 0 19 475708 9
PACK ISBN: 978 0 19 475714 0

Printed in Hong Kong

10 9 8 7 6 5 4 3 2 1

Acknowledgments:

Cover art:
Hans Hofmann
Combinable Wall I and II
1961
Oil on canvas
Overall: 84-1/2 x 112-1/2 inches
University of California, Berkeley Art Museum: Gift of the artist.

The publisher would like to thank the following for their permission to
reproduce photographs: © PhotosIndia.com/Index Imagery, Inc., v; © Kevin
Radford/SuperStock, 1; © Christian Liewig/TempSport/Corbis, 2; © Richard
Ross/The Image Bank/Getty Images, 5; © Clive Mason/Staff/Getty Images, 8;
Courtesy NASA, 13; © Central Press/Stringer/Hulton Archive/Getty Images,
14; Courtesy NASA, 17; Courtesy NASA 17; Courtesy NASA, 20; © Ansel
Adams Publishing Rights Trust/CORBIS, 25; © GABRIEL BOUYS/Staff/AFP/Getty
Images, 26; © Ansel Adams Publishing Rights Trust/CORBIS, 29; Illustrated by
Woodshed, 32; © Jung Yeon-Je/Staff/AFP/Getty Images, 37; © Johannes Eisele/
Staff/AFP/Getty Images, 38; Illustrated by Woodshed, 41; © CJ Entertainment/
courtesy Everett Collection, 44; © Walter Bibikow/Index Imagery, Inc., 49;
© Dalgleish Images/Alamy, 50; Illustrated by Woodshed, 53; © Ralph Krubner/
Index Imagery, Inc., 56; © Jeff Greenberg/Index Imagery, Inc., 61; © Stephen
Venables/Royal Geographical Society/Alamy, 62; Illustrated by Woodshed,
65; © Mark Perlstein/Time Life Pictures/Getty Images, 65; © Mike Watson
Images/SuperStock, 68; © ImageState/Alamy, 73; © Mireille Vautier/Alamy,
74; © Walter Bibikow/Jon Arnold Images/Alamy, 77; © David R. Frazier
Photolibrary, Inc./Alamy, 77; © Peter M. Wilson/Alamy, 77; © Felix Stensson/
Alamy, 80; © Motoring Picture Library/Alamy, 85; © Terrafugia, 86; © Bill Lai/
Index Imagery, Inc., 89; © Lockheed Martin, 92.

The authors and publisher would like to acknowledge the following
individuals for their invaluable input during the development of this series:
Russell Frank, Pasadena City College, CA; Maydell Jenks, Katy Independent
School District, TX; Maggie Saba, King Abdulaziz University in Jeddah, Saudi
Arabia; Grant Trew, Oxford University Press, Japan; Heidi Vande Voort Nam,
Department of English Education, Chongshin University, Seoul, South Korea.

CONTENTS

TO THE TEACHER

Welcome to *Panorama Listening 3,* a listening skills book for intermediate level students. *Panorama Listening 3* combines high-interest listening passages from the content areas with a strong vocabulary strand and extensive listening skills practice to prepare students for the challenges of academic listening.

As in the companion reading strand, each of the eight main units in *Panorama Listening* consists of three chapters, and each chapter has a thematically-linked listening passage. The first passage is about a person, the second on a related place, and the third on a related concept or event. The topics in each unit are related to those in the corresponding unit of *Panorama Reading*.

The book begins with an introductory unit, Essential Listening Skills, that presents and practices the basic listening skills needed for academic success.

WHAT IS IN EACH UNIT?

Before You Listen
This opening page introduces the theme of the unit. The questions and photographs can be used to activate students' prior knowledge and stimulate discussion before listening.

Prepare to Listen
This section introduces the topic of the chapter. The questions and photographs encourage students to become engaged in the topic while sharing their own thoughts and experiences.

Word Focus 1
This activity introduces students to new or unfamiliar words that they will hear in the listening passage. Students match the words with simple definitions.

Make a Prediction
This activity encourages students to make a prediction about a specific piece of information that appears in the listening passage. The aim is to motivate students to listen to the passage to find the answer.

Listening Passage
Each listening in Book 3 is about 600 words. The language is carefully graded so that students gain confidence in listening.

Check Your Comprehension
These multiple-choice and true/false questions check students' understanding of the passage. The questions include key skills such as understanding the main idea, listening for details, and listening for inference.

Word Focus 2
In this activity students are introduced to 10 target vocabulary items related to the topic of the chapter in the context of a reading passage. Students have already heard these words in the listening passage. After reading the passage, students match the words with definitions. These vocabulary items will be useful for the discussion activity that follows.

Discuss the Theme
In this section of the chapter students are given the opportunity to discuss questions related to the topic of the chapter and the information they learned from the reading and listening passage.

Vocabulary Review
This section reviews the vocabulary presented in the unit. It includes a wide variety of activities, such as **Words in Context** (filling in the gaps), **Wrong Word** (finding the word that doesn't fit the group), and **Word Families** (choosing the part of speech that fits). These activities help students use the new words as part of their active vocabulary.

Wrap It Up
This final section of the unit gives students the opportunity to extend the knowledge they have acquired from the listening and reading passage and their discussions to the world outside the classroom.

For the **Project Work** students are asked to conduct a survey, prepare a presentation, or attend presentations. This can be done individually, in pairs, or in small groups.

For the **Internet Research** students are asked to research a topic related to the listening passage. This activity integrates a number of skills and encourages students to work independently.

The **Essential Listening Skills: Answer Key and Explanations,** a **Vocabulary Index,** and a list of **Common Irregular Verbs** can be found at the back of the book for easy reference.

The *Audio Scripts, Answer Key,* and eight *Unit Tests* are available in the *Answer Key and Test Booklet* that accompanies *Panorama Listening 3.*

ESSENTIAL LISTENING SKILLS

WHAT TO DO BEFORE YOU LISTEN

MUSIC AND INTELLIGENCE

Music for baby's ears

PREVIEW AND PREDICT

Before you listen, preview and predict. When you preview, you look at the title, pictures, vocabulary, and questions. When you predict, you make logical guesses about content.

A. Look at the picture only. (Don't read the caption yet.) Answer these questions.

1. Describe what you see. _____

_____

2. What things can you guess or predict about the content of the listening passage from the picture? _____

_____

B. Now read the title and caption. Answer these questions.

1. What information does the title tell you? _____

2. What information does the caption tell you? _____

3. What type of music is the baby listening to? _____

4. Do you think the baby can play music? _____

✔ Look at page 97 for the explanations.

C. Now preview the vocabulary.

1. This passage is probably going to discuss music for babies. What words do you expect to hear? Make a list and share it with a classmate.

2. Now look at the list of words below. You will hear these words in the listening passage. Were any of your words in this list?

benefit – advantage; good or useful effect of something

classical music – traditional, not modern music

media – television, radio, and newspaper used as a means of communication

Mozart – a classical music composer who lived from 1756–1791

relaxation – what you do in order to rest or relax

a study – scientific research into a particular subject

D. Make a prediction about the listening.

Researchers studied babies to learn about intelligence.

a. True   **b.** False

🎧 Now listen to a lecture. Check your prediction.

✔ Look at page 97 for the explanations.

WHAT TO DO WHILE YOU LISTEN

MAIN IDEA

Every listening passage has a main idea. This is the most important topic or most general idea. Preview the main idea question below.

E. 🎧 Now listen to the lecture again. Identify the main idea in question 1. Circle your answer.

MAIN IDEA

1. What is the main topic?
   A. research about early childhood development
   B. studies about the link between babies and intelligence
   C. whether listening to classical music increases intelligence
   D. whether listening to classical music makes you smarter than listening to popular music

✔ Look at page 97 for the explanation.

DETAIL

Every passage has many smaller, specific pieces of information that tell you more about the main idea. These are called details. Read the questions below.

F. 🎧 **Listen to the audio again and answer the questions. Circle your answers.**

DETAIL

2. The research took place in
   A. 1993
   B. a college
   C. a music class
   D. a music recording company

3. The students who listened to Mozart
   A. did better on all their tests
   B. did better on part of a test
   C. were more intelligent than other students
   D. all of the above

4. According to the lecture, which of the following is **not** true?
   A. The researchers did not say anything about intelligence.
   B. Listening to classical music makes children more intelligent.
   C. Other researchers have not been able to get the same results.
   D. The students who listened to Mozart had better scores in spatial reasoning.

5. What did people remember about news reports on the research results?
   A. Students got higher scores only in a task related to folding paper.
   B. The effects of listening to classical music only lasted for 10 minutes.
   C. Students got higher scores on a test after they listened to classical music.
   D. Students may have scored higher because they enjoyed the music and were more alert.

6. Which of these is most likely to increase results on math tests?
   A. only piano practice
   B. folding paper
   C. classical music
   D. studying music

7. Parents bought CDs with classical music because
   A. the governor wanted them to
   B. they believed that would make their children smarter
   C. they wanted their children to play classical music
   D. all of the above

8. The speaker thinks that music education is
   A. not important
   B. a beneficial activity
   C. the only way to increase intelligence
   D. all of the above

✔ Look at page 98 for the explanations.

INFERENCE

> You can use details to make logical guesses. These logical guesses are called inferences. Often you have to think about information you heard in different parts of the passage and then piece the information together.

G. Listen to the passage and answer the questions. Circle your answers.

INFERENCE

9. The entrepreneurs started selling CDs with classical music because they wanted to help children be more intelligent.
   A. True
   B. False

10. This lecture is probably part of
    A. a math course
    B. a teacher education course
    C. a course in a medical school
    D. a business course

✔ Look at page 99 for the explanations.

WORDS IN CONTEXT, PART 1

> In every passage, you will often hear words that are unfamiliar to you. Listen for clues in the sentence or in nearby sentences to help you understand words in context.

H. Circle the answers with the same meaning as the words in boldface. Then underline the clues that helped you.

1. All they said was that listening to Mozart increased students' **performance** on a test of spatial reasoning.
   A. the state of being perfect or without fault
   B. the ability to notice or understand something
   C. the way in which you do something, especially how successful you are

2. Well, of course **entrepreneurs** saw this as a big opportunity. They started putting together CDs with classical music, mostly Mozart, and sold them to parents.
   A. people who work to find their way through difficult places
   B. people who start businesses and often take risks to become successful
   C. people who manage things without preparation using what they have on hand

3. So, is there a **link** between music and intelligence? No, at least not according to current research.
   A. connection
   B. computer
   C. chain

WORDS IN CONTEXT, PART 2

Sometimes the speaker gives a clue by defining the words while speaking. The speaker might include a definition, for example, or a synonym.

4. Underline the definition of *spatial reasoning.*

Spatial reasoning means being able to figure out where things go and to follow patterns.

5. Underline the part of the sentence that helps define *enjoyment effect.*

Some of these researchers attributed the improvement to the "enjoyment effect." That is, the students might have been more alert because they had just had a pleasant experience.

6. Underline the part of the sentence that helps define *misinterpreted.*

And it got misinterpreted. People didn't hear, "its effect lasted for 10 minutes." They heard, "the students got higher scores on a test."

7. Underline an example of a claim.

People made a lot of claims such as "This CD is designed to improve your baby's mind."

✔ **Look at page 99 for the explanations.**

UNIT 1

SPORTS
SOCCER

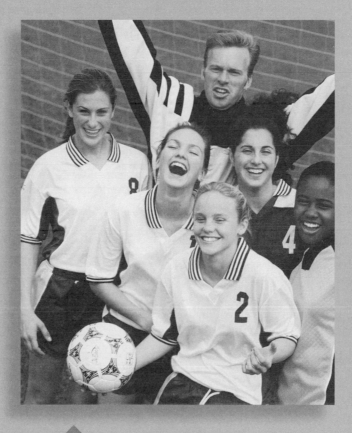

▲ A soccer team

BEFORE YOU LISTEN

Answer these questions.

1. What do you think is the most popular sport in the world?

2. Have you ever played soccer? Do you watch soccer?

3. What are the basic rules of the game?

1

CHAPTER 1
GEORGE WEAH: LIBERIA'S SOCCER STAR

George Weah, soccer player

PREPARE TO LISTEN

Look at the picture above. Discuss these questions.

1. Have you heard of George Weah? Who are some other famous soccer players?

2. What does it take to be a good soccer player?

WORD FOCUS 1

Match the words with their definitions.

election	round	war-torn
humanitarian	score	

1. a person who works to help other people _____
2. get points, in a game or on a test _____
3. one part of a competition, used in politics and sports _____
4. severely affected by war inside a country's borders _____
5. the time for choosing leaders such as president _____

MAKE A PREDICTION

George Weah became the president of Liberia.

a. True   **b.** False

🎧 **Now listen to a radio news story about George Weah. Check your prediction.**

🎧 **Listen to the audio again and answer the questions. Circle your answers.**

MAIN IDEA

1. What is the main topic?
   A. George Weah: player, politician, humanitarian
   B. George Weah: the newest Liberian politician
   C. George Weah: helping the children of the world
   D. George Weah: coach of a Liberian soccer team

DETAIL

2. George Weah grew up
   A. in a poor neighborhood
   B. in Monrovia
   C. with his grandmother
   D. all of the above

3. Weah's first team was
   A. Yaoudé Thunder
   B. The Invincible Seven
   C. The Invincible Eleven
   D. The Liberian Thunder

4. Who did Weah play with when he won the Golden Ball award?
   A. Paris St. Germain
   B. AC Milan
   C. Chelsea
   D. Manchester City

5. When did FIFA name Weah "World Player of the Year"?
   A. in 1966
   B. in 1988
   C. in 1994
   D. in 1995

6. According to the report, the money from Weah's CD went to
   A. children's soccer teams
   B. UNICEF
   C. children's programs in Liberia
   D. children's programs throughout Africa

7. Which of the following is **not** true?
   A. The Lone Stars won all of their games.
   B. Weah coached the Lone Stars.
   C. Weah played for the Lone Stars.
   D. The Lone Stars are a Liberian team.

8. Which of the following is true about Weah's campaign?
   A. Some Liberians felt he had lived away for too many years.
   B. He made promises to the rich people of his country.
   C. He had the most votes in the final election.
   D. all of the above

INFERENCE

9. Why did Weah help child soldiers?
   A. He had been a child soldier.
   B. They needed help to return to society.
   C. He wanted to be president.
   D. They were good soccer players.

10. Why is Ellen Johnson-Sirleaf mentioned?
    A. She was a famous soccer player.
    B. She became the president of Liberia.
    C. She was Weah's grandmother.
    D. none of the above

Read this e-mail message about the report on George Weah. Notice the bold words. Then match the bold words to their definitions below.

To: WNFQ Radio
Subject: Your Report on George Weah

Thank you for your report on the **extraordinary** George Weah. In my opinion, he should be president of Liberia today. Weah became a **politician** because he wanted to serve his country. Unfortunately, his plan to **run for** president was not successful. He got the most votes in the first round of the elections. But Ellen Johnson-Sirleaf won in the final round. Most people know that he was a very successful soccer player in Europe. He had **contracts** with some of the most successful European soccer teams. He **supported** a soccer team in Liberia. He talked about his ideas during his presidential **campaign**. He promised great things for the country. But many people thought that a soccer player didn't have enough experience to be a leader. But they were wrong. Here's why:

Weah's grandmother **raised** him in Monrovia's poorest area. He never forgot the poor people that he grew up with. This is why he **cares about** his country. Weah showed that he could be a good leader. He left soccer. He came home to help his fellow Africans. For example, he helped child soldiers return to **society**. He helped them readjust to their own cultures and communities. He also **coached** a Liberian soccer team. Because of his work with the team, they won many games. They gave Liberians something to be proud of. These are some of the reasons I think that Weah should be president of Liberia.

A.

1. campaign ___   **a.** written agreements for work
2. cares about ___ **b.** very special
3. coached ___   **c.** an effort to become elected
4. contracts ___   **d.** is worried about; is interested in
5. extraordinary ___ **e.** trained a team in a sport

B.

1. politician ___   **a.** the culture of an area or country
2. raised ___   **b.** took care of a child
3. run for ___   **c.** provided money for something
4. society ___   **d.** be one of the people in an election
5. supported ___   **e.** a person who is in or who wants to be in an elected position

Read these questions and discuss them with a partner.

1. Do you think a soccer player can be a leader of a country? Why or why not?

2. What kind of person makes a good leader?

CHAPTER 2
MARACANÃ STADIUM

Maracanã Stadium

PREPARE TO LISTEN

Look at the picture above. Discuss these questions.

1. What do you think happens at this stadium?
2. Why might this stadium be famous?

WORD FOCUS 1

Match the words with their definitions.

field	rivals	sportswriter	World Cup
founder	spectators	standing room	

1. an international soccer competition held every four years _____
2. an area of land used for sports _____
3. a person who starts something such as a business _____
4. people who watch a game _____
5. a place to watch in a stadium while standing _____
6. people or teams who compete against you; opponents _____
7. a person whose job is to write about teams and athletes _____

MAKE A PREDICTION

Maracanã Stadium is an important part of Italian soccer history.

a. True   **b.** False

🎧 **Now listen to a radio interview about Maracanã Stadium. Check your prediction.**

🎧 **Listen to the audio again and answer the questions. Circle your answers.**

MAIN IDEA

1. What is the main topic?
   - **A.** when Maracanã Stadium was built
   - **B.** which teams play at Maracanã Stadium
   - **C.** Maracanã Stadium's role in soccer history
   - **D.** Pelé's role in Brazilian soccer history

DETAIL

2. Maracanã Stadium was finished in
   - **A.** 1938
   - **B.** 1948
   - **C.** 1950
   - **D.** 1960

3. Brazil won the 1950 World Cup.
   - **A.** True
   - **B.** False

4. The original name of Maracanã Stadium was
   - **A.** Maracanã Stadium
   - **B.** Municipal Stadium
   - **C.** Mario Filho Stadium
   - **D.** The Rio Newspaper Stadium

5. The name *Maracanã* came from
   - **A.** the person who built the stadium
   - **B.** a person who started a newspaper
   - **C.** a team that plays in the stadium
   - **D.** the neighborhood of the stadium

6. How many people can watch a game at Maracanã sitting down?
   - **A.** 77,720
   - **B.** 103,022
   - **C.** 200,000
   - **D.** 700,000

7. Which of the following is **not** true?
   - **A.** Pelé first played at Maracanã Stadium.
   - **B.** Frank Sinatra gave a concert at Maracanã Stadium.
   - **C.** Paul McCartney scored a goal at Maracanã Stadium.
   - **D.** The Rolling Stones performed at Maracanã Stadium.

8. What does *aura* mean?
   - **A.** a special feeling
   - **B.** a bad feeling
   - **C.** a special place
   - **D.** a bad place

INFERENCE

9. American football is the same as soccer.
   - **A.** True
   - **B.** False

10. Most Brazilians want to
    - **A.** build a new Maracanã Stadium
    - **B.** get rid of Maracanã Stadium
    - **C.** move Maracanã Stadium
    - **D.** keep Maracanã Stadium

Read this e-mail message about the radio interview. Notice the bold words. Then match the bold words to their definitions below.

To: WNFQ Radio
Subject: Your Interview about Maracanã Stadium

Thank you for your **terrific** interview on Maracanã Stadium. I thought it was excellent. Like many in the radio **audience**, I am a big soccer fan. And I agree with your guest sportswriter. She said that the stadium is an important part of soccer history. This **expresses** my feelings exactly.

Maracanã is one of the biggest stadiums in the world. As your guest **mentioned**, it held 200,000 spectators for the 1950 World Cup. That was the largest number of spectators ever at a sporting event. **Construction** has changed the stadium since then. But that **record** still stands. The **capacity** of the stadium is now around 77,000. That's because more spectators are seated now. Standing room still **brings** the number **up to** over 100,000 people.

I visited Maracanã last year. I understand why there are **protests** about changing it. People want to improve the stadium for future games. I hope they never **tear** it **down** completely. I hope Maracanã will continue to be an important part of soccer history in the future.

A.

1. audience ___
2. brings (the number) up to ___
3. capacity ___
4. construction ___
5. expresses ___

a. shows an opinion or feelings
b. makes the total
c. the largest amount that something can hold
d. the people watching an event
e. the act of building something

B.

1. mentioned ___
2. protests ___
3. record ___
4. tear down ___
5. terrific ___

a. the most ever
b. destroy; remove completely
c. actions that show that a group disagrees with something; demonstrations
d. said
e. excellent; extremely good

DISCUSS THE THEME

Read these questions and discuss them with a partner. Share your ideas with the class.

1. Have you ever been in a big stadium? Describe the experience.

2. Would a stadium be a good place to see a concert? Why or why not?

CHAPTER 3
THE WORLD CUP

Celebrating the win in the World Cup

PREPARE TO LISTEN

Look at the picture above. Discuss these questions.

1. What are these people doing?
2. Soccer is an international sport. What are some other international sports?

WORD FOCUS 1

Match the words with their definitions.

defeated	match	tied	upsets
host	sources	trophy	

1. places where information comes from _____
2. a person or group who invites others to some event _____
3. a statue or cup that the winner of a competition gets _____
4. having the same score _____
5. wins of games when losses were expected _____
6. won a game against; was the winner over _____
7. an organized game _____

MAKE A PREDICTION

The first official soccer game was in 1950.

a. True   **b.** False

🎧 **Now listen to part of a lecture on the World Cup. Check your prediction.**

🎧 **Listen to the audio again and answer the questions. Circle your answers.**

MAIN IDEA

1. What is the main topic?
   A. The World Cup is an international soccer competition.
   B. The World Cup is the name of an international soccer team.
   C. The World Cup is an international soccer organization.
   D. The World Cup is held in different countries.

DETAIL

2. People in ancient China played a game similar to soccer.
   A. True
   B. False

3. When did soccer become an Olympic sport?
   A. in 1739
   B. in 1900
   C. in 1908
   D. in 1930

4. Who hosted the first World Cup?
   A. France
   B. Uruguay
   C. Argentina
   D. Yugoslavia

5. The winner of the World Cup keeps the solid gold cup for four years.
   A. True
   B. False

6. What was special about the 2002 World Cup?
   A. It was the first one hosted in Asia.
   B. North Korea defeated Italy.
   C. Hungary made 27 goals.
   D. The final game ended in a tie.

7. What is special about Gerd Müller?
   A. He was the oldest player in World Cup history.
   B. He was the top scorer in World Cup history.
   C. He made the fastest goal in World Cup history.
   D. He made the most goals in 1954.

8. Which of the following is **not** true?
   A. Pelé was the youngest player in World Cup history.
   B. Roger Milla was the oldest player in World Cup history.
   C. The most goals in one game were by Germany.
   D. Hakan Sukur made the fastest goal in World Cup history.

INFERENCE

9. There were no World Cup games during World War II.
   A. True
   B. False

10. Which of the following is true?
    A. Brazil has won fewer World Cups than Italy.
    B. Brazil has won more World Cups than Germany.
    C. Italy has won more World Cups than Germany.
    D. none of the above

Read this student's summary of the lecture. Notice the bold words. Then match the bold words to their definitions below.

The lecture was on the history of the World Cup. The World Cup is an international soccer **competition**. Soccer as a game grew in **popularity** after the 1908 Olympics. In the 1920s FIFA president Jules Rimet dreamed of a World Cup. But it didn't become a **reality** until 1930. More than ten countries **participated in** the first World Cup. Some of the countries that played were Paraguay, Bolivia, France, and Uruguay. Uruguay was the **champion** in the first World Cup. They won the final game against Argentina.

The World Cup **takes place** every four years. In the past, it **alternated** between Europe and the Americas. But 2002 was an exception. Instead of being in Europe or the Americas, the 2002 World Cup took place in Asia. Japan and Korea co-hosted.

Besides **fame**, the World Cup champion receives a solid gold trophy. There are many interesting World Cup **statistics**. Some of the facts included who the oldest and youngest players were. Another was the player with the most goals in the history of the competition. It was Gerd Müller. It will be interesting to see who will **break** his **record** and make more goals in the future.

A.
1. alternated ___
2. break (a) record ___
3. champion ___
4. competition ___
5. fame ___

a. do something better or faster than before
b. the winner
c. changed from one to another
d. an organized event which people try to win; a contest
e. being known by many people

B.
1. participated in ___
2. popularity ___
3. reality ___
4. statistics ___
5. takes place ___

a. something that really exists
b. happens
c. took part in an activity; played in
d. information collected in numbers about things
e. accepted; common

DISCUSS THE THEME

Read these questions and discuss them with a partner. Share your ideas with the class.

1. Are sports important? Why or why not?

2. Are international competitions such as the Olympics or the World Cup important? Why or why not?

VOCABULARY REVIEW

WORDS IN CONTEXT

Fill in the blanks with words from each box.

capacity	construction	protests	reality

1. Jules Rimet's World Cup dream became a _____ in 1930.
2. _____ on the new stadium started in 2005, but the builders didn't finish until 2008.
3. There were a lot of _____ when they tore down the old stadium.
4. The _____ of the new stadium is about 150,000 people.

champion	coached	popularity	takes place

5. The _____ of the first World Cup was Uruguay. They won against Argentina.
6. Soccer's _____ continues to grow. People around the world watch or play the sport.
7. The World Cup _____ in a different country each time.
8. George Weah _____ the Lone Stars, and he also played for them.

WRONG WORD

One word in each group does not fit. Circle the word.

1. stadiums   spectators   fans   audience
2. founder   politician   final   humanitarian
3. terrific   war-torn   popular   extraordinary
4. run for   coach   take the field play
5. World Cup   election   FIFA   host
6. match   score   soccer   politician

WORD FAMILIES

Fill in the blanks with words from each box.

| expression (*noun*) | expressive (*adjective*) | express (*verb*) |

1. The speaker tried to _____ her opinion, but people weren't listening.
2. The speaker wasn't very _____, so her speech wasn't very interesting.
3. She used an English _____ that I didn't understand.

| competition (*noun*) | competitive (*adjective*) | compete (*verb*) |

4. It helps to be _____ if you want to be a good soccer player.
5. I went to Maracanã Stadium and saw an exciting _____ between two soccer teams.
6. Many teams _____ in the World Cup, but only two teams play in the final.

WRAP IT UP

PROJECT WORK

Survey two people outside of class about sports. Ask them the following questions:

- What is your favorite sport to watch?
- What is your favorite sport to play?
- Are sports important? Why or why not?

Present your findings to the class. Discuss the results with your classmates.

INTERNET RESEARCH

Go online and find information about a sport that interests you. Find answers to the following questions:

- What is the history of the sport?
- Where do people play the sport? What equipment do they need?
- Who are some famous players of the sport? What are some interesting statistics?

Print a photo relating to the sport, if you can. Present your information to the class.

ASTRONOMY
SPACE EXPLORATION

▲ The Russian Soyez Spacecraft

BEFORE YOU LISTEN

Answer these questions.

1. How long ago did humans first go into space? Give some examples of early space travel.

2. How has space travel changed since then?

3. Would you like to travel into space? Why or why not?

CHAPTER 1
VALENTINA TERESHKOVA: COSMONAUT

◀ Valentina Tereshkova, 1937–

PREPARE TO LISTEN

Look at the picture above. Discuss these questions.

1. What country is Valentina Tereshkova from?
2. Why do you think she is famous?

WORD FOCUS 1

Match the words with their definitions.

cosmonaut	orbit	seagull	transmission
manned space flight	parachute	solo flight	

1. a bird that lives near the ocean _____
2. a large piece of cloth that lets a person fall slowly from an airplane _____
3. a flight in which the pilot flies alone _____
4. the Russian word for *astronaut* _____
5. circle around a planet _____
6. a space flight operated by a person instead of a computer _____
7. sending a message _____

MAKE A PREDICTION

Valentina Tereshkova was the first person to go into space.

a. True   **b.** False

🎧 **Now listen to this radio show about Valentina Tereshkova. Check your prediction.**

🎧 **Listen to the audio again and answer the questions. Circle your answers.**

MAIN IDEA

1. What is the main topic?
   A. Tereshkova orbited the Earth.
   B. Tereshkova's flight was the longest space flight made by a woman.
   C. Tereshkova made important contributions to her country and the world.
   D. Tereshkova was an important person in the Soviet government.

DETAIL

2. According to the speaker, what award did Tereshkova receive?
   A. the Greatest Woman Achiever of the Century Award
   B. the First Woman in Space Award
   C. the Greatest Woman in the World Award
   D. the Most Honored Woman of the Century Award

3. Tereshkova went into space in
   A. 1937
   B. 1961
   C. 1963
   D. 1999

4. Tereshkova's background was highly valued because
   A. her father was a World War II hero
   B. she was a parachutist
   C. she was active as a young Communist
   D. all of the above

5. How many space flights did Tereshkova make?
   A. 1
   B. 3
   C. 48
   D. 58

6. Which of the following is **not** true?
   A. "Chaika" was Tereshkova's radio call name.
   B. "Chaika" was the name of Tereshkova's daughter.
   C. "Chaika" means *seagull* in Russian.
   D. There was a watch called "Chaika."

7. Who chose Tereshkova to be the first female cosmonaut?
   A. President Khrushchev
   B. The International Women of the Year Association
   C. The Communist Party
   D. Cosmonaut Yuri Gagarin

8. Why did doctors think Tereshkova's daughter, Elena, might not be normal?
   A. Tereshkova was in space for six months.
   B. Both parents had been in space.
   C. Tereshkova got sick from her space flight.
   D. Elena was born in space.

INFERENCE

9. Only men and women who were pilots could become cosmonauts.
   A. True
   B. False

10. What did Tereshkova do between 1969 and 1999?
    A. She served her country at home and around the world.
    B. She stayed at home and had more children.
    C. She became president of the Soviet Union.
    D. She worked for the company that sold Chaika watches.

Read this e-mail message about the report on Valentina Tereshkova. Notice the bold words. Then match the bold words to their definitions below.

To: "At the Minute" radio show
Subject: Your program about Valentina Tereshkova

I found your show about Valentina Tereshkova very interesting. I can see why some people think Tereshkova should be the Greatest Woman **Achiever** of the Century. I understand that she was **announced** the winner yesterday. She has accomplished much. This is especially true because her **background** was very ordinary. Her family was working class, she was not well educated, and she was not a pilot. It is remarkable that she was **recruited** to be a cosmonaut and that she **holds** the record for the longest solo flight for a woman in space. However, I can think of many other women more **qualified** to receive this honor, women who have contributed even more than Tereshkova.

I would recommend Helen Keller for this award. She could not see or hear. However, she achieved more than most people who have **normal** sight and hearing. She led an **active** life. She gave speeches and showed others what people with physical challenges can achieve.

There are many other women who could have received this award. There are women who were **experts** in science and medicine. Some of them saved thousands of lives through their discoveries. My **selection** of Helen Keller, however, is based on what she achieved and her contributions to the world.

A.

1. achiever ___
2. active ___
3. announced ___
4. background ___
5. experts ___

  a. the type of family, social class, and education you come from
  b. describing someone who participates in an organization
  c. someone who gains success through effort or skill
  d. people with special knowledge or skill
  e. made something known publicly

B.

1. holds ___
2. normal ___
3. qualified ___
4. recruited ___
5. selection ___

  a. got someone to join something
  b. has, used for a record or a title
  c. the act of being chosen
  d. formed in the usual way
  e. skilled or experienced enough to do something

DISCUSS THE THEME

Read these questions and discuss them with a partner.

1. What do you think it was like to be the first man or woman in space?

2. Who would you choose as the Greatest Woman Achiever of the last century? Why?

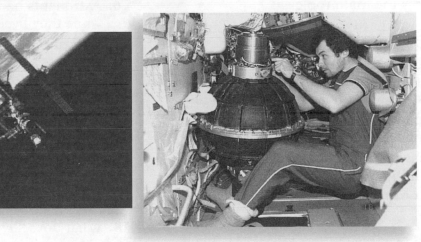

Mir Space Station

Inside the Mir Space Station

PREPARE TO LISTEN

Look at the pictures above. Discuss these questions.

1. What do you know about the Mir Space Station? Is it still in space?
2. What are space stations used for? What do people who work in them do?

WORD FOCUS 1

Match the words with their definitions.

dehydrated	gravity	modules
exercise equipment	link-up	quarters

1. machines used for physical activity indoors _____
2. the place provided for a person to live, usually not in a house _____
3. something joined together by a computer for communication _____
4. describing food from which all the water is removed _____
5. units that are part of something bigger _____
6. the natural force that makes things fall to the ground _____

MAKE A PREDICTION

Astronauts and scientists from different countries stayed on the Mir Space Station.

a. True   **b.** False

🎧 **Now listen to a news report about life on a space station. Check your prediction.**

🎧 **Listen to the audio again and answer the questions. Circle your answers.**

MAIN IDEA

1. What is the main topic?
   A. It was hard to get astronauts and scientists to go to the Mir Space Station.
   B. Living on Mir was not comfortable, but astronauts adjusted to being there.
   C. Spending too much time on Mir was unhealthy for some astronauts.
   D. Having little contact with astronauts' families was the hardest part of living on Mir.

DETAIL

2. Mir was used as a space station between
   A. 1948 and 1981
   B. 1978 and 2001
   C. 1980 and 2000
   D. 1986 and 2001

3. Most astronauts and scientists stayed on Mir
   A. less than one month
   B. between one and three months
   C. more than three months
   D. between three months and one year

4. People living on Mir slept
   A. in beds attached to the floor
   B. in beds attached to the walls
   C. in sleeping bags attached to the floor
   D. in sleeping bags attached to the walls

5. The Russians
   A. launched Mir into space
   B. helped the U.S. launch Mir into space
   C. were the only people to use Mir
   D. all of the above

6. Astronauts had to dress in space suits while they lived on Mir.
   A. True
   B. False

7. What does the speaker mean by "as homey as possible"?
   A. forgetting about home
   B. giving a home to someone
   C. making a living area comfortable
   D. belonging to a specific group of people

8. What does "living spaces" refer to?
   A. the reasons people cannot live in space
   B. the areas where people live on a space station
   C. the places where there is no air on the space station
   D. the types of living things that may be in space

INFERENCE

9. The Mir Space Station is no longer orbiting Earth.
   A. True
   B. False

10. Life on the space station was difficult because
    A. there was not much space to live or work
    B. communicating with family was difficult
    C. the food was not very good
    D. all of the above

Read this excerpt from a magazine interview with a Mir astronaut. Notice the bold words. Then match the bold words to their definitions below.

After Mir was **launched** in 1986, numerous astronauts and scientists visited and worked on the space station, **generally** staying one to three months. The **exception** was cosmonaut Sergei Avdeyev. During three trips to Mir, he stayed a total of 748 days. In an interview, one of the cosmonauts talked about what it was like to live in space.

Question: What was it like to live in space for so long?
It was exciting, challenging, and sometimes boring. Few people have the chance to see Earth from space. It's a beautiful planet. However, the challenging part was **adjusting** to the small quarters. Being away from family was also a **hardship**. We counted the days until those **reunions** with our families. I especially **regret** the time away from my children. They've grown up to be wonderful people, so perhaps this didn't **affect** them too much.

Question: What was boring about Mir?
Mostly doing the same things over and over again. We were responsible for **maintaining** the space station. Our activities were limited. And there was little variety in the food we ate.

Question: Did the people living on Mir **get along with** each other?
We got along with each other pretty well. People who go to space are chosen very carefully, and they were usually there for fewer than three months.

Question: Why is Mir no longer in space?
The station got old. It was built to last five years, and it was used for 15 years. It took a lot of maintenance to keep everything running well.

A.
1. adjusting ___
2. affect ___
3. exception ___
4. generally ___
5. get along with ___

   a. getting used to new conditions
   b. have a friendly relationship with someone
   c. usually
   d. cause a problem
   e. a person or thing that is not included

B.
1. hardship ___
2. launched ___
3. maintaining ___
4. regret ___
5. reunions ___

   a. difficulty or problems
   b. sent into space
   c. keeping something in good condition
   d. coming together after a separation
   e. feel sorry about something

DISCUSS THE THEME

Read these questions and discuss them with a partner. Share your ideas with the class.

1. What do you think is the greatest hardship on a space station? Why?

2. Imagine you are going to a space station for three months. What would you take with you?

CHAPTER 3
SPACE DEBRIS

◄ A computer drawing of Earth and space debris

PREPARE TO LISTEN

Look at the picture above. Discuss these questions.

1. There is a lot of debris, or junk, in space. Where do you think it comes from?

2. What problems might this space debris cause?

WORD FOCUS 1

Match the words with their definitions.

calculate	meteorites	satellites
chunks	rockets	sonic boom

1. electronic equipment sent into space to travel around a planet _____
2. pieces of rock in outer space _____
3. find an answer using mathematics _____
4. large pieces of something _____
5. a very loud noise when something goes faster than the speed of sound _____
6. tube-shaped vehicles used to send things into space _____

MAKE A PREDICTION

Space debris has injured people on Earth.

a. True   **b.** False

🎧 **Now listen to a radio interview with a university student. Check your prediction.**

🎧 **Listen to the audio again and answer the questions. Circle your answers.**

MAIN IDEA

1. What is the main topic?
   A. what space debris is and how it affects spacecraft and Earth
   B. where space debris comes form
   C. how dangerous space debris is to humans
   D. how space debris can be removed from space to protect spacecraft and humans

DETAIL

2. Space debris does **not** include
   A. meteorites
   B. nuts, bolts, and paint chips
   C. pieces of satellites and spacecraft
   D. astronauts' gloves

3. Who is responsible for most of the debris in space?
   A. the U.S. and the former Soviet Union
   B. the European Space Agency and the U.S.
   C. the former Soviet Union
   D. none of the above

4. When space debris falls to Earth, it usually lands in water.
   A. True
   B. False

5. Approximately how many pieces of debris are in space?
   A. fewer than 300 pieces
   B. around 500 pieces
   C. more than 4,000 pieces
   D. more than 40,000 pieces

6. According to the speaker, the chunk that fell in Texas
   A. was the size of a school bus
   B. was a large fuel tank
   C. weighed 5,800 pounds (2,610 kilos)
   D. all of the above

7. Small pieces don't usually burn up when they fall to Earth.
   A. True
   B. False

8. According to the speaker, space debris causes the greatest danger to
   A. spacecraft
   B. people on Earth
   C. buildings on Earth
   D. the oceans because of pollution

INFERENCE

9. Which of these can cause a sonic boom?
   A. any object falling to the ground
   B. a jet traveling faster than the speed of sound
   C. a car traveling very fast
   D. a satellite floating around in space

10. What types of space debris can be dangerous?
    A. tools and astronauts' gloves
    B. chunks of space stations
    C. pieces of satellites and rockets
    D. all of the above

Read this student's journal entry about the interview. Notice the bold words. Then match the bold words to their definitions below.

This morning I heard a really interesting interview on the radio. It was about space junk. I found out that space junk is also called space debris. It's all the stuff that's left in space when old space stations or satellites fall apart or rockets **explode**.

There's a great **variety** of junk out there in space. It can be things like paint chips. And it can even be things lost in space like astronauts' tools and gloves. When things explode, the debris **floats around** in space. Some pieces can **collide** with spacecraft. They can cause a lot of damage. Other pieces fall to the Earth's **surface**. There were some **spectacular cases** of debris falling to Earth, including two **identical** fuel tanks. They each weighed 580 pounds (264 kilograms). Fortunately, no one on the ground was injured.

Researchers **estimate** that there are more than 4,000 pieces of man-made debris in space. That number may not be **accurate** because it's impossible to **document** an exact number. I wonder how they count space debris.

A.
1. accurate ___
2. collide ___
3. document ___
4. estimate ___
5. explode ___

a. hit something very hard while moving
b. make a record of something
c. guess about the size or amount of something
d. exact
e. blow up with a loud noise

B.
1. floats around ___
2. identical ___
3. spectacular cases ___
4. surface ___
5. variety ___

a. the outside part of something
b. a number of different kinds of things
c. exactly the same
d. very amazing situations or examples
e. moves slowly

DISCUSS THE THEME

Read these questions and discuss them with a partner. Share your ideas with the class.

1. Do you think there will be more or less space debris in the future? Why?

2. How could we remove debris from space?

VOCABULARY REVIEW

WORDS IN CONTEXT

Fill in the blanks with words from each box.

| background | collides | exception | recruited |

1. In the past, most astronauts were pilots. The female cosmonauts were the _____.

2. The Russian space program _____ women with parachute jumping experience because there were no female pilots.

3. Today, many of the astronauts have a/an _____ in engineering.

4. When space debris _____ with spacecraft, there is damage because the debris hits with great force.

| affected | estimate | got along with | holds the record |

5. Astronauts and scientists on Mir usually _____ each other since there were few disagreements.

6. Valentina Tereshkova still _____ for having the longest solo flight of any woman astronaut.

7. Sergei Avdeyev's long stay in space _____ his heart. When he returned to Earth, it took a year for him to recover.

8. Space programs _____ that there are more than 4,000 pieces of space junk.

WRONG WORD

One word in each group does not fit. Circle the word.

1. destroy   damage   explode   maintain
2. accurate   exact   perfect   estimated
3. document   collide   crash   hit
4. separation   reunion   division   explosion
5. happiness   comfort   hardship   peace
6. identical   different   strange   unusual

WORD FAMILIES

Fill in the blanks with words from each box.

selection (*noun*)	selective (*adjective*)	select (*verb*)

1. Space programs are _____ about the people they recruit.
2. The final _____ of Tereshkova was made by President Khrushchev.
3. The Russian space program had to _____ the female cosmonauts from 400 women who applied.

variety (*noun*)	various (*adjective*)	vary (*verb*)

4. Space debris comes from a great _____ of objects.
5. Objects of _____ sizes have fallen from space; some were as large as a school bus.
6. The amount of time visitors stayed on Mir Space Station would _____ from one to three months.

WRAP IT UP

PROJECT WORK

Survey 2–4 people outside of class to find out what they know about space exploration.

- Who was the first person to go into space? The first woman? The first American?
- Do you think governments should spend money on space exploration?
- Would you like to travel into space? Ask for a reason.
- Will we ever live on the moon? On Mars? Ask for a reason.

Present your findings to the class. Discuss the results with your classmates.

INTERNET RESEARCH

Go online and find information about space exploration. Try to find information about at least one of the following:

- What astronauts or scientists from your country have gone into space?
- What were the modules of Mir used for? What did scientists on Mir study?
- Which countries have left debris in space? What types and amount?

Print a photo, if you can. Present your information to the class.

PHOTOGRAPHY
FINE ART PHOTOGRAPHY

"Bridal Veil Fall" by Ansel Adams, 1927

Answer these questions.

1. Describe the picture. What do you see?

2. What do you think the photographer wanted us to think?

3. What are photos used for? Think of as many uses as possible.

CHAPTER 1

SEBASTIÃO SALGADO: PHOTOGRAPHER

Sebastião Salgado,
1944–

PREPARE TO LISTEN

Look at the picture above. Discuss these questions.

1. Describe the picture. What do you see?
2. What types of photographers can you think of?

WORD FOCUS 1

Match the words with their definitions.

agency	drought	photo essay
documentary photography	natural disasters	photojournalist

1. a person who works reporting news using photos, especially in a magazine
   _____

2. photos that show facts or information about a particular subject _____
3. a group of photos that tell a story _____
4. events in nature that cause a lot of harm or damage _____
5. a business that provides a particular type of service, such as travel, photography, modeling, etc. _____
6. a long period of weather that is too dry _____

MAKE A PREDICTION

Sebastião Salgado is a fashion photographer.

a. True　　**b.** False

🎧 **Now listen to a lecture about Sebastião Salgado. Check your prediction.**

🎧 **Listen to the audio again and answer the questions. Circle your answers.**

MAIN IDEA

1. What is the main topic?
   A. Sebastião Salgado is a photojournalist who takes photos of rich people.
   B. Sebastião Salgado is a photojournalist whose photos tell important stories.
   C. Sebastião Salgado worked with Doctors Without Borders.
   D. Sebastião Salgado is a photojournalist who is interested in workers.

DETAIL

2. Salgado's photographs are in color.
   A. True
   B. False

3. What was Salgado's first profession?
   A. photographer
   B. journalist
   C. economist
   D. architect

4. Where was Salgado born?
   A. Brazil
   B. France
   C. the U.S.
   D. Angola

5. According to the speaker, where did Salgado's interest in photography begin?
   A. in Paris
   B. in Africa
   C. in Brazil
   D. none of the above

6. Salgado donated the money from two books to
   A. Doctors Without Borders
   B. UNICEF
   C. the people of Rwanda
   D. 43 countries

7. Which of the following is **not** the subject of Salgado's photos?
   A. hunger in Africa
   B. people who work with their hands
   C. changes in cities
   D. migration of birds

8. What is Salgado doing today?
   A. working as an economist in London
   B. working with his wife at their company in Paris
   C. working for a photographic agency in Brazil
   D. working as a photojournalist in Brazil

INFERENCE

9. Why was Salgado with Doctors Without Borders?
   A. He was documenting the famine.
   B. He was working as a doctor.
   C. He was an economist studying crops in Africa.
   D. He was writing for a newspaper.

10. Why does the speaker say that Salgado's photos are "hard to look at"?
    A. It is difficult to find them.
    B. The images aren't very clear.
    C. They can make you feel bad.
    D. The bright colors hurt your eyes.

Read this student's summary of the lecture. Notice the bold words. Then match the bold words to their definitions below.

The lecture was on the photographer Sebastião Salgado. Salgado started out as an **economist**. He had a job with an international coffee **organization**. His job for this group introduced him to poor countries and he traveled to places in Africa.

Salgado wanted to show what he saw. So he started taking pictures. At first, photography was a hobby. But he finally left his job. He started taking pictures **full time**. He has had many shows and has **published** several books of his photography. Today, he works with his wife. She studied **architecture**. But she no longer designs buildings. Instead, she helps him run their photography agency in Paris.

In my opinion, Salgado is one of the best **photographers** in the world. Many photographers take good pictures. But Salgado also tells us important information about the world. For example, he shows us **images** of people who have no food. He shows us images of people who were forced to move from their homes. These pictures of **famine** and **migration** tell us a lot. They show us how many people in the world today are living.

People have different **reactions** to his work. His work makes some people sad. But at the same time it makes people glad that someone is telling an important story about the world.

A.

1. architecture ___
2. economist ___
3. famine ___
4. full time ___
5. images ___

a. the whole normal period of work
b. pictures or descriptions in a book, movie, or painting
c. a person who studies how countries use resources and money
d. the study of how buildings are planned and built
e. a lack of food in a large area that can cause the death of many people

B.

1. migration ___
2. organization ___
3. photographers ___
4. published ___
5. reactions ___

a. what you do or say after you see something; responses
b. people who take pictures with a camera
c. a group of people who do something together
d. the act of moving from one place to go live and work in another
e. prepared and printed something and made it available to the public, especially a book

DISCUSS THE THEME

Read these questions and discuss them with a partner.

1. Would you like to be a documentary photographer? What would you document?

2. Can a photo help to change the world? Explain your answer.

◀ "Moon and Half Dome" by
Ansel Adams, 1960

PREPARE TO LISTEN

Look at the picture above. Discuss these questions.

1. What do you see in the picture?

2. What do know about Yosemite Valley? Where do you think it is?

WORD FOCUS 1

Match the words with their definitions.

redwood trees	meadows	wilderness
cliffs	waterfalls	

1. extremely large, tall trees that grow in California _____
2. fields of grass _____
3. rivers of water that fall down from a mountain or a high rock _____
4. an area of land with very few signs of human life _____
5. high, very steep areas of rock _____

MAKE A PREDICTION

Yosemite was Ansel Adams' favorite subject.

a. True   **b.** False

🎧 **Now listen to part of a lecture on the photography of Ansel Adams. Check your prediction.**

🎧 **Listen to the audio again and answer the questions. Circle your answers.**

MAIN IDEA

1. What is the main topic?
   A. Ansel Adams took the photograph "Moon and Half Dome."
   B. Yosemite is a beautiful national park.
   C. Ansel Adams' photographs of Yosemite are in black and white.
   D. Ansel Adams' photographs show a special relationship with Yosemite.

DETAIL

2. Which of the following is **not** true?
   A. Yosemite is in the Sierra Nevada Mountain range.
   B. Yosemite was the first national park.
   C. Yosemite is in eastern California.
   D. Yosemite is a small park.

3. Ansel Adams first saw Yosemite when he was
   A. 8 years old
   B. 14 years old
   C. 19 years old
   D. 31 years old

4. Why does the speaker say, "He felt his duty was to protect Yosemite"?
   A. Adams felt that it was his job to take care of Yosemite.
   B. Adams felt that protecting Yosemite was a good job.
   C. The owners of the park made Adams feel responsible for it.
   D. Yosemite made Adams feel happy.

5. "Half Dome, Evening, Olmstead Point" is a photograph of a waterfall.
   A. True
   B. False

6. In "Half Dome, Evening, Olmstead Point," we see peaks. Another word for *peak* is
   A. valley
   B. moon
   C. mountain top
   D. sky

7. "Yosemite Fall, Profile" shows a waterfall in the far distance.
   A. True
   B. False

8. How did Adams feel about nature?
   A. He felt that it was dead.
   B. He felt that it is was frightening.
   C. He felt that it was not important.
   D. He felt that it was a living thing.

INFERENCE

9. What is "landscape photography"?
   A. photographs of families outside
   B. photographs of scenes in nature
   C. photographs of farmers at work
   D. photographs of Earth from space

10. No one lived in Yosemite before it was a national park.
    A. True
    B. False

Read this student's summary of the lecture. Notice the bold words. Then match the bold words to their definitions below.

We discussed photographer Ansel Adams and his favorite **subject**, Yosemite Valley. Yosemite Valley was Adams' favorite place to photograph. He had a very close **relationship** with it. He lived there most of his life. He cared deeply about Yosemite. Yosemite **inspired** Adams.

Adams loved the **beauty** of Yosemite. He recorded its attractive **features** in many of his photographs. Some of these features include tall cliffs, wide meadows, and beautiful waterfalls.

Adams also had a feeling of **awe** about Yosemite. You can see it in his pictures. Everything is grand. The mountains are tall. The waterfalls are powerful. He shows his **respect** for nature in his photos. Adams placed a very high value on the natural world. He was in awe of the **miracle** of nature. To Adams, nature is amazing and wonderful.

His photo of a **thundering** waterfall is an example. You can almost hear the loud noise that it makes. You can almost feel the water hit your face. You feel like you are a part of the waterfall. Adams wants us to **identify with** nature, and this kind of photograph helps us to feel that.

A.

1. awe ___   **a.** feel connected with someone or something
2. beauty ___   **b.** important or noticeable parts of something; characteristics
3. features ___   **c.** the quality that gives pleasure to the senses; attractiveness
4. identify with ___ **d.** gave ideas to someone
5. inspired ___   **e.** a feeling of respect and either fear or admiration

B.

1. miracle ___   **a.** making a very loud noise
2. relationship ___   **b.** a wonderful and very unusual event that is impossible to explain
3. respect ___   **c.** the feelings that you have when you admire someone or something
4. subject ___   **d.** the connection between two or more things
5. thundering ___   **e.** the thing that is shown or talked about; topic

DISCUSS THE THEME

Read these questions and discuss them with a partner. Share your ideas with the class.

1. Do you think Ansel Adams' photos would be as powerful in color? Why or why not?

2. What is your relationship with nature? Are you like Ansel Adams? In what ways?

CHAPTER 3
PHOTO IMAGING SOFTWARE

◀ Before and after images

PREPARE TO LISTEN

Look at the pictures above. Discuss these questions.

1. Compare the pictures. What are the differences?
2. Why do people change photographs?

WORD FOCUS 1

Match the words with their definitions.

dating websites	event	scene
digital images	faked	serious

1. pictures that are made with computers _____
2. something that takes places, especially something important _____
3. made something that seemed real but was not _____
4. places on the Internet where people can meet each other _____
5. bad; causing worry _____
6. what you see around you in a particular place _____

MAKE A PREDICTION

People do not change news photos.

a. True   **b.** False

🎧 **Now listen to a radio interview about imaging software. Check your prediction.**

🎧 **Listen to the audio again and answer the questions. Circle your answers.**

MAIN IDEA

1. What is the main topic?
   A. using software to change photographs
   B. photojournalists fired for changing news photos
   C. computer software for thinner people
   D. famous people in altered photos

DETAIL

2. Photo software can
   A. make people look thinner
   B. change hair and eye color
   C. remove spots from a person's skin
   D. all of the above

3. What did the photojournalist add to the war photo?
   A. He added guns.
   B. He added smoke.
   C. He added bombs.
   D. He added fire.

4. The speaker says, "But lately, we're hearing about more serious uses of image altering." Why does the speaker say *serious uses*?
   A. People in the fake images were unhappy.
   B. The fake images may cause harm.
   C. The fake images make people sad.
   D. People in the fake images were late.

5. What did both newspapers do when they learned about the fake photos?
   A. They apologized to the photojournalists.
   B. They published more altered photographs.
   C. They fired the photographers.
   D. They did nothing.

6. It is impossible to tell when people fake photos.
   A. True
   B. False

7. Which of the following is **not** mentioned?
   A. Women like to make themselves look thinner.
   B. Men like to add more hair.
   C. Both men and women make themselves look taller.
   D. Both men and women fake photos on dating websites.

8. Which of the following statements is true?
   A. Photo imaging software is fairly difficult to use for most people.
   B. Only professional photographers can change photos.
   C. Newspapers sell photo imaging software.
   D. Most photos are impossible to change even with software.

INFERENCE

9. Someone dressed up like John Kerry and Jane Fonda for the fake photo.
   A. True
   B. False

10. Why might people change their photos on dating websites?
    A. They don't care about how they look.
    B. They want to look better.
    C. They think they look good.
    D. none of the above

Read this e-mail about the news report on photo imaging software. Notice the bold words. Then match the bold words to their definitions below.

To: WNFQ Radio
Subject: Your Report on Photo Software

Thanks for your great report on photo imaging software. I'm a **professional** photographer. My job is taking pictures. So I know all about image **altering**. Changing photos is common in **advertising**. Advertisers use imaging software to make people and things in ads look better. They remove **blemishes** and other kinds of marks. They make products look nicer and models look prettier. That's OK. As your guest said, it's cheaper than **cosmetic surgery**. It's also a lot less painful than having your features changed by a doctor!

But it is absolutely *not* OK. to alter images in news photos. This is dishonest. We expect ads to be **misleading**. Most people know that ads don't tell the truth. But the news *must* tell the truth. A photographer showed a **candidate** with an actress. This hurt his chances to be elected. That's unfair. Another photographer showed soldiers **mistreating** prisoners for a newspaper story. The soldiers never hurt the prisoners. This is also unfair. I'm glad the newspapers **fired** the photographers who altered the photos. People who do this *should* lose their jobs. Photographers who do this owe us an **apology**!

A.

1. advertising ___   **a.** marks on the skin
2. altering ___   **b.** making something different in some way, but without changing it completely
3. apology ___   **c.** information used to persuade people to buy something
4. blemishes ___   **d.** a spoken or written statement that you are sorry for something you have done
5. candidate ___   **e.** a person who wants to be elected to a particular position

B.

1. cosmetic surgery ___   **a.** said that someone could no longer work at a job, usually because of something bad
2. fired ___   **b.** giving a wrong idea or impression; not telling the truth
3. misleading ___   **c.** doing something that requires skill and training as a job
4. mistreating ___   **d.** a medical treatment to change someone's appearance
5. professional ___   **e.** behaving badly or cruelly to a person or an animal; hurting

DISCUSS THE THEME

Read these questions and discuss them with a partner. Share your ideas with the class.

1. What examples of image altering have you heard of?

2. Is it OK to alter photos for a dating website? Why or why not?

VOCABULARY REVIEW

WORDS IN CONTEXT

Fill in the blanks with words from each box.

features	identify with	published	subjects

1. Adams' images help us to _____ nature. They help us to feel part of the natural world.

2. Adams shows us the beautiful _____ of Yosemite, such as the tall cliffs and the waterfalls.

3. Salgado _____ many books of his photographs, so now everyone can see his work.

4. Salgado and Adams chose very different _____ for their photographs. Salgado photographs people; Adams photographed nature.

advertising	misleading	professional	relationship

5. Salgado first became interested in photography as a hobby. Later he became a _____ photographer.

6. Adams had a close connection with the natural world. Most of his pictures show his _____ with nature.

7. You expect altered images in _____. Information about products is often not true.

8. You don't expect fake images of real events. You don't expect these images to be _____.

WRONG WORD

One word in each group does not fit. Circle the word.

1. meadows   waterfalls   digital images   redwoods

2. economist   photojournalist   candidate   apology

3. images   photo essay   documentary   drought

4. famine   miracle   awe   beauty

5. agency   organization   features   group

6. wilderness   cliffs   architecture   valleys

WORD FAMILIES

Fill in the blanks with words from each box.

beauty (*noun*)	beautiful (*adjective*)	beautify (*verb*)

1. The group wanted to _____ the park, so they removed all the garbage.
2. There are several _____ waterfalls in Yosemite National Park.
3. The natural _____ of Yosemite inspired Ansel Adams' photographs.

inspiration (*noun*)	inspirational (*adjective*)	inspire (*verb*)

4. Salgado's _____ images teach us to respect humanity.
5. Salgado got the _____ for his photographs from his trips to Africa.
6. Salgado's photographs can _____ people to help others.

WRAP IT UP

PROJECT WORK

Survey 2–4 people outside of class about altering photographs. Ask the following questions:

- Is it OK to alter news photos? Why or why not?
- Is it OK to alter advertising images? Why or why not?
- Is it OK to alter a photo of yourself? Why or why not?
- When is it OK to alter a photo?

Present your findings to the class. Discuss the results with your classmates.

INTERNET RESEARCH

Go online and find information about a photo by Ansel Adams or Sebastião Salgado. Find answers to the following questions:

- Which photographer took the photo? When and where was it taken?
- Does the photo have a title? What does the photo show?
- What does it tell you about the subject? What does it tell you about the photographer?
- How does it make you feel?

Print the photograph, if you can. Present your information to the class.

CULTURAL STUDIES
KOREAN FILMS

Korean movie poster

Answer these questions.

1. What is your favorite movie?

2. What types of movies do you like to watch?

3. Have you seen any Korean films? If you have, what were they about?

CHAPTER 1
IM KWON TAEK: KOREAN FILMMAKER

◀ Filmmaker Im Kwon Taek, 1936–

PREPARE TO LISTEN

Look at the picture above. Discuss these questions.

1. Who is your favorite filmmaker?
2. What types of films does he or she make?

WORD FOCUS 1

Match the words with their definitions.

action films	contemporary	film festival	theme
classics	director	melodramas	

1. things that are important and have a value that will last _____
2. of the present time; modern _____
3. the person who tells the actors and crew what to do in a movie or play _____
4. an event at which many movies are shown, often held yearly in the same place

   _____
5. ideas that are developed or repeated in the work of a filmmaker or artist _____
6. films that deal with a lot of emotions and feelings _____
7. films in which a lot of dangerous, exciting things happen _____

MAKE A PREDICTION

As a child, Im Kwon Taek dreamed of being a filmmaker.

a. True   **b.** False

🎧 **Now listen to a class discussion on Korean filmmaker Im Kwon Taek. Check your prediction.**

🎧 **Listen to the audio again and answer the questions. Circle your answers.**

MAIN IDEA

1. What is the main topic?

A. Im Kwon Taek's road to success

B. how the film "Deserted Widow" was made

C. the history of Korean film

D. the films that Im Kwon Taek directed

DETAIL

2. Im Kwon Taek started making films in

A. 1936

B. 1962

C. 1973

D. 1983

3. Im Kwon Taek received formal training to become a director.

A. True

B. False

4. What did the lecturer mean by "put food on the table"?

A. cook a meal

B. put a table into the kitchen

C. earn money to feed a family

D. feed people who are sitting at the kitchen table

5. At the beginning of his career, Im Kwon Taek worked as a filmmaker because

A. his father was a filmmaker

B. he wanted to make money

C. he was an artist

D. all of the above

6. In the first 10 years of his career, Im Kwon Taek made about

A. 5 films

B. 10 films

C. 50 films

D. 100 films

7. How did Im Kwon Taek feel about his early films?

A. He was dissatisfied with them.

B. He was proud of them.

C. He hadn't made enough films.

D. He wanted more filmgoers to like his movies.

8. The model for the main character in "The Deserted Widow" was probably

A. his mother

B. his wife

C. his sister

D. his grandmother

INFERENCE

9. Im Kwon Taek's career shows that

A. serious art films can be successful

B. commercial filmmakers can also be directors of serious films

C. it isn't necessary to have formal training to become a film director

D. all of the above

10. Why is nature important in Im Kwon Taek's films?

A. He wants people to move to the country.

B. It relates to Korean cultural identity.

C. Women plant flowers and vegetables.

D. He shows people how to be farmers.

Read this excerpt from an article in a magazine about Im Kwon Taek. Notice the bold words. Then match the bold words to their definitions below.

After the commercial success of the movie "Sopyonje" in 1983, the **renowned** film director Im Kwon Taek had the freedom to make only serious art films. Im, a former **laborer**, learned to direct films by making films. However, he made many films that he was **dissatisfied** with before "Sopyonje." In fact, his first serious film, "The Deserted Widow," was made ten years earlier in 1973. Until "Sopyonje," however, he was still also directing action films and melodramas in order to make money.

"The Deserted Widow" is about the life of a young woman, Nam Han-boong. Her **suffering** was typical of many Koreans living in the **post-war** period in the early 1950s. She was separated from her husband and traveled to Busan to find him. Along the way, she suffered many hardships. Im admits that his mother served as a model for the subject of this film. The film shows many of the same **struggles** his mother had during and after the war. Many film **critics** praised the film, but others believed the movie was too antiwar.

Remarkably, even in a film about war, Im always found a way to include something that he has become famous for—his beautiful filming of the Korean **landscape**. The **shots** of the **countryside** that we see in "The Deserted Widow" are of a land mostly destroyed by war. Im, however, is still able to show us the beauty that was once in that landscape.

A.
1. countryside ___   **a.** the natural features that you see outdoors
2. critics ___   **b.** a person who does hard, physical work
3. dissatisfied ___   **c.** the land which is away from towns and cities, consisting of farms, woods, etc.
4. laborer ___   **d.** not satisfied; unhappy
5. landscape ___   **e.** people whose job is to give opinions about something

B.
1. post-war ___   **a.** existing or happening after the end of a war
2. renowned ___   **b.** famous and talked about by a lot of people
3. shots ___   **c.** experiencing something very bad
4. struggles ___   **d.** photographs or parts of film in a movie
5. suffering ___   **e.** great efforts

DISCUSS THE THEME

Read these questions and discuss them with a partner.

1. Describe a recent movie that you enjoyed. Do you prefer action films, melodramas, or serious art films?

2. Have you ever made a video? If yes, describe it. What kind of camera did you use? What was easy or hard about doing it?

CHAPTER 2
PUSAN INTERNATIONAL FILM FESTIVAL

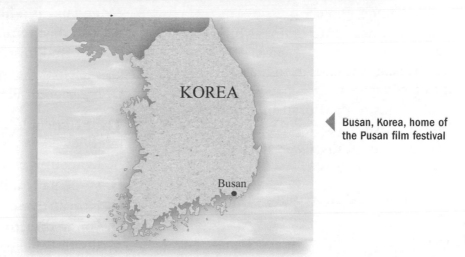

Busan, Korea, home of
the Pusan film festival

PREPARE TO LISTEN

Look at the map above. Discuss these questions.

1. Are you familiar with any film festivals? If you are, what do you know about them?

2. What do you think the purpose of a film festival is? What kinds of films are shown?

WORD FOCUS 1

Match the words with their definitions.

featured	filmgoers	perform
filmfest	monk	

1. a man who lives in a religious community _____
2. included something or someone as an important part _____
3. people who go to movies _____
4. a short form of the term *film festival* _____
5. play in front of an audience _____

MAKE A PREDICTION

Film festivals usually feature only contemporary films.

a. True   **b.** False

🎧 **Now listen to an interview at a film festival. Check your prediction.**

🎧 **Listen to the audio again and answer the questions. Circle your answers.**

MAIN IDEA

1. What is the main topic?
   A. what the Pusan International Film Festival is
   B. why Busan was chosen to have this film festival
   C. who comes to the Pusan International Film Festival
   D. how this film festival was started

DETAIL

2. The Pusan festival started in
   A. 1967
   B. 1970
   C. 1976
   D. 1996

3. The purpose of the festival is to
   A. promote the making of Korean movies
   B. feature Asian films
   C. show the films of young and older filmmakers
   D. all of the above

4. The Pusan International Film Festival has become more popular every year.
   A. True
   B. False

5. *Pansori* is the name of a Korean
   A. film
   B. song tradition
   C. actor
   D. director

6. The film "Sopyonje" was hard to make because
   A. it had to be filmed entirely in the countryside
   B. it had to be filmed in a Buddhist temple
   C. it was difficult to find actors to perform *pansori*
   D. it took 10 years to film everything

7. "Mandala" is a film about
   A. Buddhist temples
   B. two Buddhist monks
   C. the *pansori* song tradition
   D. a period of Korean history

8. The two people who were interviewed were
   A. living in Korea
   B. students at a film school
   C. Korean-American actors
   D. young directors with films in the festival

INFERENCE

9. What is **not** true about the films shown at the Pusan festival?
   A. Some are older classics.
   B. Many are new, contemporary films.
   C. No one has seen any of them before.
   D. Some are historically important.

10. Why might movie fans go to a film festival?
    A. to see serious art films
    B. to see famous actors and directors
    C. to meet other movie fans
    D. all of the above

Read this newspaper report about the Pusan International Film Festival. Notice the bold words. Then match the bold words to their definitions below.

Pusan International Film Festival

The Pusan **International** Film Festival was held in Busan, Korea this month. The fest first started in 1996. It has only gotten better each year. There are film festivals in other parts of the world that are older and more famous. However, this film festival is the **leading** festival for Asian films. Serious movie fans like to go to Pusan because the festival **represents** the best examples of Asian film.

Originally, the festival was in the coastal city of Busan. In recent years, the festival **outgrew** the city and festival events began to move north of Busan to the **suburb** of Haeundae. Contemporary films by young directors are an important part of the festival. Young movie fans are always interested in learning about newer **styles** of film. But **historically** important films will always be featured at Pusan. This is because many people who come to the festival are filmgoers who appreciate the films of directors like Im Kwon Taek. These older directors tend to make films about the **purity** and beauty of life in an earlier period. However, young people often have different reactions to these films because their life experiences are different. Therefore, it is important to have a film festival that appeals to young and old moviegoers. The Pusan International Film Festival does this. I believe Pusan will continue to be an important film festival in Asia for many years to come, **promoting** the best of Asian films.

A.

1. historically ___
2. international ___
3. leading ___
4. originally ___
5. outgrew ___

a. in the beginning
b. best or very important
c. describing history or the study of history
d. involving two or more countries
e. became too big for something

B.

1. promoting ___
2. purity ___
3. represents ___
4. styles ___
5. suburb ___

a. is a picture, sign, or example of something
b. something untouched by bad things
c. helping something to happen or develop; encouraging
d. the ways that things are done, built, etc.
e. an area where people live that is outside the city

DISCUSS THE THEME

Read these questions and discuss them with a partner. Share your ideas with the class.

1. What older films do you enjoy watching? What newer films do you like?

2. Imagine you are organizing a film festival. Where would it be? What types of movies would you show? Explain your reasons.

CHAPTER 3
THE KOREAN WAVE

A shot from a recent Korean movie

PREPARE TO LISTEN

Look at the picture above. Discuss these questions.

1. How do you decide what movies to watch?
2. Do you watch soap operas? Describe the ones you have watched.

WORD FOCUS 1

Match the words with their definitions.

dubbed	rusty	subtitles
province	soap opera	wave

1. a continuing story about the lives of a group of people, on television or radio
   _____

2. translated words at the bottom of the picture on television or in a movie _____

3. describing the changing of actors' voices in a movie to a different language
   _____

4. a sudden increase or spread of something _____

5. describing a skill that is of poor quality because you have not used it for a long time
   _____

6. one of the main parts into which some countries are divided _____

MAKE A PREDICTION

Korean soap operas are popular in Japan.

a. True   **b.** False

🎧 **Now listen to a conversation between two students. Check your prediction.**

🎧 **Listen to the audio again and answer the questions. Circle your answers.**

MAIN IDEA

1. What is the main topic?
   A. Korean film, TV, and video are becoming popular outside of Korea.
   B. Asian film classes study the films of Im Kwon Taek.
   C. Korean music videos are becoming popular with Korean Americans.
   D. Korean soap operas are very popular in Japan.

DETAIL

2. Jin speaks some Korean.
   A. True
   B. False

3. How many films did Jin see at the festival?
   A. 2
   B. 5
   C. 6
   D. 8

4. Cholla is the name of
   A. a Korean film
   B. a Korean province
   C. a Korean soap opera
   D. a character in a Korean film

5. In the passage, the expression *soaps* refers to
   A. things used to wash clothes and dishes
   B. a type of Korean movie
   C. a type of MTV K video
   D. a short form of *soap operas*

6. Many Japanese like to watch Korean soap operas because
   A. they like stories about true love
   B. the stories have happy endings
   C. they remind them of simpler times
   D. all of the above

7. Which of the following is **not** true?
   A. Jin didn't know about MTV Korea until her friend mentioned it.
   B. MTV Korea shows videos made by Korean Americans.
   C. Korean Americans can use the MTV Korea website to talk to each other.
   D. MTV Korea is similar to MTV in the U.S.

8. Jin mostly uses MTV Korea to listen to music.
   A. True
   B. False

INFERENCE

9. Jin mentions the film about the woman Chunhyang because
   A. the actress was also in a Korean soap opera
   B. Jin met the actress who played her at the film festival
   C. it was filmed in Japan
   D. the theme is similar to stories in Korean soap operas

10. According to this discussion, it is probably true that
   A. only older Korean Americans are interested in Korean culture
   B. Korean Americans are not interested in their Korean cultural identity
   C. there is a growing wave of interest in Korean culture
   D. the wave of interest in Korea has not spread to Japan

Read these comments on the Internet. Notice the bold words. Then match the bold words to their definitions below.

Six months ago, I hadn't heard of Korean soaps. Now, I can't stop watching them! I usually don't like **romantic** stories. I also noticed that Korean **versions** of soaps don't continue for years like in the U.S. I like that. I'm writing **from a distance**. I have no connection with Korea. I just like these soaps!

Posted by: Mary in LA/November 5

What a **coincidence**! I recently discovered Korean soaps, too. They're dubbed into Chinese here in San Francisco. My Chinese-speaking parents never miss "Jewel in the Palace." My mom and I often talk about the show. Nothing on American TV **moves** me like this show does. The main character overcomes **obstacles**, and she maintains her beliefs even if she might be **punished** for them.

Posted by: SanFran Connie/November 6

Hello, I am writing from Japan. I also watch these Korean shows. You use the word "soaps." Are soaps the same as "soap operas" in English? The Koreans have been **exporting** Korean soap operas to Japan for several years. I think we like them because they show a less **modernized** society. In these shows people's feelings are important.

Posted by: Hiroko/November 10

Hi, Hiroko. You're right. The word "soaps" means "soap operas" **for short**. What Korean soaps do you watch in Japan?

Posted by: Mary in LA/November 12

A.

1. coincidence ___
2. exporting ___
3. for short ___
4. from a distance ___
5. modernized ___

a. used to refer to a short form for something
b. sending something to another country, usually for sale
c. describing something that is no longer old
d. two things happening at the same time by chance
e. from far away

B.

1. moves ___
2. obstacles ___
3. punished ___
4. romantic ___
5. versions ___

a. causes someone to have strong feelings about something
b. caused someone to suffer for doing something wrong
c. things that make it difficult to go somewhere or do something
d. new or different forms of something
e. having a quality that makes you think about love

DISCUSS THE THEME

Read these questions and discuss them with a partner. Share your ideas with the class.

1. Do you watch movies from other countries? Do you prefer to watch them with subtitles or dubbed? Why?

2. Why do you think people like soap operas?

VOCABULARY REVIEW

Fill in the blanks with words from each box.

concidence	critics	exporting	outgrew

1. Korea is now _____ films, soap operas, and videos to many other countries.

2. It is interesting that Korean films and soap operas became popular at about the same time. Is this a/an _____?

3. The film festival _____ the city and moved to a suburb.

4. Filmmakers and actors pay attention to what _____ say about their films and acting.

dissatisfied	obstacles	rusty	versions

5. Characters in soap operas always face terrible _____, but there is usually a happy ending.

6. American _____ of TV soap operas continue for years and years, but Korean soaps usually go on for a shorter time.

7. When people don't study a language for a while or don't travel to other countries, their language skills often become _____.

8. Im Kwon Taek became _____ with his early commercial films. He wanted to make serious art films instead.

WRONG WORD

One word in each group does not fit. Circle the word

1. romantic   featured   sentimental   melodramatic
2. dubbed   subtitled   original   translated
3. recent   modernized   historical   contemporary
4. director   movie fan   filmgoer   audience
5. suffering   struggles   hardships   purity
6. shots   melodrama   soap opera   action film

WORD FAMILIES

Fill in the blanks with words from each box.

| critic (*noun*) | critical (*adjective*) | criticize (*verb*) |

1. People will probably _____ the director for the ending of the film.
2. The film _____ didn't like the new movie at all.
3. She was very _____ of the ending.

| origin (*noun*) | originally (*adjective*) | originate (*verb*) |

4. Did the *pansori* song tradition _____ in the Cholla province of Korea?
5. Jin's father _____ came from the Cholla province.
6. No one is sure what the _____ of the soap opera is.

WRAP IT UP

PROJECT WORK

Ask 2–4 people outside of class about foreign films, soaps, and music. Ask the following questions:

- What foreign films have you seen recently? Describe what they were about.
- Do you ever watch soap operas? Why or why not? Do you have a favorite soap opera? What is it?
- What popular music do you listen to? Do you just listen to music, or do you watch music videos?

Present your findings to the class. Discuss the results with your classmates.

INTERNET RESEARCH

Go online and find information about one of the following:

- the films shown at the most recent Pusan International Film Festival
- a list of all of the films made by Im Kwon Taek or another director you like
- information about popular Korean soaps in Asia, the U.S., or other countries
- where to find MTV Korea on the web

Print a photograph, if you can. Present your information to the class.

HISTORY
ALASKA

The Alaskan landscape

BEFORE YOU LISTEN

Answer these questions.

1. What do you know about the state of Alaska?

2. What country separates Alaska from the rest of the United States?

3. What is the weather like in Alaska?

CHAPTER 1
EARLY EUROPEAN EXPLORERS IN ALASKA

◀ A sailing ship

PREPARE TO LISTEN

Look at the picture above. Discuss these questions.

1. Describe the picture. When were these ships used?
2. Have you ever been on a sailing ship like the one in the picture?

WORD FOCUS 1

Match the words with their definitions.

banks	expedition	herds
czar	fur	panel

1. soft, thick hair covering the bodies of many animals _____
2. the title used by kings in Russia _____
3. a group of people invited to discuss something and answer questions _____
4. large numbers of animals that live together _____
5. the ground along the sides of a river _____
6. a long trip for a special purpose, often for exploration _____

MAKE A PREDICTION

The first European explorers to Alaska were from England.

a. True   **b.** False

🎧 **Now listen to a lecture about European explorers in Alaska. Check your prediction.**

🎧 **Listen to the audio again and answer the questions. Circle your answers.**

MAIN IDEA

1. What is the main topic?
   A. European explorers and the Alaskan fur trade
   B. European exploration of Alaska in the 17th and 18th centuries
   C. European explorers' search for the Northwest Passage
   D. European exploration for oil in Alaska in the 17th and 18th centuries

DETAIL

2. Caribou are animals that live together in a huge group.
   A. True
   B. False

3. Which of these is **not** mentioned as a use for animal skins?
   A. blankets
   B. boats
   C. bowls
   D. tents

4. Bering Island was named after
   A. a Russian czar
   B. a Russian sea captain
   C. a Native Alaskan
   D. a fur trader

5. According to the passage, Spanish explorers made maps of the coast.
   A. True
   B. False

6. What does *passage* mean in the term *Northwest Passage*?
   A. a ticket to travel on a ship
   B. a way through something
   C. a section from a piece of writing
   D. the passing of time

7. What does "Captain Cook's ships headed north to Alaska" mean?
   A. The ships traveled north toward Alaska.
   B. Captain Cook stayed at the front of his ship.
   C. From Alaska the ships traveled farther north.
   D. The ship at the head of the group was from Alaska.

8. Which of the following is **not** true?
   A. Captain Cook explored the South Pacific.
   B. Spanish explorers named several places in Alaska.
   C. The English set up the first village in Alaska.
   D. The Russian-American Company traded fur.

INFERENCE

9. What is probably true about the Spanish explorers to Alaska?
   A. They were the first Europeans to sail to Alaska.
   B. They were expert hunters.
   C. They found the Northwest Passage.
   D. They were excellent mapmakers.

10. When Natalya Shelikhov died,
    A. the fur trading stopped
    B. her husband ran the company
    C. Alaska still belonged to Russia
    D. all of the above

Read this newspaper article about Captain Cook. Then match the bold words to their definitions below.

Captain James Cook, Explorer

If Captain James Cook lived today, he would surely be exploring the unknown corners of space. In the 1700s, men like Cook explored the world on wooden sailing ships.

James Cook was born in England in 1728. He was a **member** of the British Royal Navy. One of his jobs was to draw maps. He surveyed Newfoundland and made maps of the **land**.

In 1768, Cook led an expedition from England to the southern parts of the globe. Captain Cook **searched** unknown parts of the ocean. He made the first maps of New Zealand and Tahiti. There were **difficulties** on the voyage, but it made Captain Cook famous.

He led two more voyages. He returned to New Zealand and Tahiti, explored the South Pacific, found the islands of Hawaii, and made maps of the coast of Alaska and the Arctic Circle.

His crew brought food for many months. They also **fished** and **hunted** for food, and they found **wild** foods on the islands. Captain Cook showed that people stay much healthier on long sea voyages if they eat good foods, especially citrus fruit. This information helped improve the health of the **population** of England.

Captain Cook never **settled** in one place for long. And he never **claimed** land for England. But he studied the worlds he found as a scientist would. He was an explorer, a mapmaker, a geologist, a biologist, and many other things. But most importantly, he was a sea captain, and that is what he was famous for.

A.

1. claimed ___
2. difficulties ___
3. fished ___
4. hunted ___
5. land ___

a. followed wild animals to catch and kill them for food
b. took ownership saying it was a right or privilege
c. tried to catch fish using poles, nets, etc.
d. a large area of country
e. things that are hard to do or understand; problems

B.

1. member ___
2. population ___
3. searched ___
4. settled ___
5. wild ___

a. living or growing in natural conditions, not controlled by people
b. went to live permanently in a new place
c. a person who belongs to a specific group
d. looked very carefully to find something
e. the people who live in a particular area

DISCUSS THE THEME

Read these questions and discuss them with a partner.

1. What do you think life was like on an old sailing ship?

2. What will explorers do 250 years in the future? Use your imagination.

CHAPTER 2
ALASKAN STATEHOOD

A map of Alaska, USA

PREPARE TO LISTEN

Look at the map above. Discuss these questions.

1. Describe the map.
2. What do you think the climate of Alaska is like?

WORD FOCUS 1

Match the words with their definitions.

geologist	mountain ranges	services
miners	pipeline	statehood

1. systems that provide people with something necessary or useful in daily life _____
2. people whose job is to find minerals _____
3. a person who studies rocks and minerals _____
4. the condition of being one of the states in the U.S. _____
5. lines of mountains _____
6. tubes used for carrying liquid or gas _____

MAKE A PREDICTION

The United States took Alaska after winning a war with Russia.

a. True   **b.** False

🎧 **Now listen to a lecture about the state of Alaska. Check your prediction.**

🎧 **Listen to the audio again and answer the questions. Circle your answers.**

MAIN IDEA

1. What is the main topic?
   A. Alaska's history before the arrival of Europeans
   B. Alaska's history since the mid-1700s
   C. Alaska's history since the mid-1800s
   D. Alaska's history since the mid-1900s

DETAIL

2. What year was gold discovered in Alaska?
   A. 1800
   B. 1848
   C. 1867
   D. 1880

3. Why did people call Alaska "Seward's folly"?
   A. They thought Seward was a fool to buy Alaska.
   B. They thought Seward was a very funny person.
   C. They thought Alaskans were very foolish.
   D. They thought the Russians were foolish to sell Alaska.

4. The U.S. bought Alaska from Russia for $720 million.
   A. True
   B. False

5. Which of the following is true?
   A. Alaska became a state before it was a territory.
   B. Alaska's forests make timber a big industry.
   C. Alaska has few mineral resources.
   D. none of the above

6. Why did people want statehood after World War II?
   A. They wanted a local government.
   B. Their roads were in bad shape.
   C. They needed services such as electricity.
   D. all of the above

7. What is the 50th state in the U.S.?
   A. Alaska
   B. Iowa
   C. Hawaii
   D. Ohio

8. Which reason is mentioned for people moving to Alaska?
   A. The weather is nice all year.
   B. The cost of living is low.
   C. The laws are different.
   D. The land is majestic and beautiful.

INFERENCE

9. Why is oil sometimes called "black gold"?
   A. Oil is actually a type of gold covered by black color.
   B. Oil is valuable like gold, but it is a different color.
   C. Oil is not legal in international trade.
   D. Oil looks like the color of the night sky.

10. What is probably **not** true about the Alaska pipeline?
    A. The pipeline is around 40 years old.
    B. The pipeline is easy to maintain.
    C. The pipeline runs north to south.
    D. Oil is put on ships in Valdez.

Read this e-mail about the lectures on Alaska. Notice the bold words. Then match the bold words to their definitions below.

Hi Marvin,

Hey! I thought of you today. My history professor was talking about **immigrants** to Alaska. Didn't your great-great-grandfather go to Alaska after the Civil War?

I **discovered** that a relative long ago went to Alaska from the Philippines. He got a job on a Spanish ship in the late 1700s. He loved the **environment** in Alaska—the forests and mountains. So he stayed there. I guess you can say Spain **transported** my uncle to his new home!

Do you remember Maria from our class last year? Around 1930 her great-grandfather worked in Alaska in the salmon **industry**. The **economy** was pretty good compared to other places. Another classmate had an uncle from Japan who worked as a gold miner around 1920. He **drilled** for gold **deposits**.

It's interesting that so many people moved to Alaska even before it was a U.S. **territory**! No wonder the people in Alaska now have such **diverse** backgrounds!

So about your great-great-grandfather—did he go to Alaska to search for gold? Did he get rich? It sounds like there were a lot of interesting people exploring Alaska back then. And your great-great-grandfather was one of them! So was my uncle! Write me back soon, and tell me about your great-great-grandfather. Stay well!

A.

1. deposits ___
2. discovered ___
3. diverse ___
4. drilled ___
5. economy ___

   a. found something that nobody had found before
   b. made holes in something using a tool or machine
   c. the operation of a country's money supply, trade, and industry
   d. substances that are on or in the ground as the result of a natural process
   e. very different from each other

B.

1. environment ___
2. immigrants ___
3. industry ___
4. territory ___
5. transported ___

   a. people who came into another country to live permanently
   b. all the people, buildings, etc. that are involved in producing something
   c. took something or someone in a vehicle from one place to another
   d. an area of land that belongs to a country or ruler
   e. the natural world in which things live

DISCUSS THE THEME

Read these questions and discuss them with a partner. Share your ideas with the class.

1. What other places in the world have a lot of natural resources?

2. Where did the people in your area come from? Why did they move to your area?

CHAPTER 3
NATIVE ALASKAN CULTURES

◀ A Native Alaskan

PREPARE TO LISTEN

Look at the picture above. Discuss these questions.

1. Describe the picture.
2. How does the clothing in the picture fit the Alaskan environment?

WORD FOCUS 1

Match the words with their definitions.

ceremonial dances	gathering	shelter
every other one	legends	whiskers

1. a building or structure that gives protection; a house _____
2. not every one, but every second one _____
3. longer hairs that grow near the mouths of some animals _____
4. special dances, often religious _____
5. old stories that may or may not be true _____
6. collecting things _____

MAKE A PREDICTION

Native Alaskans all speak the same language.

a. True   **b.** False

🎧 **Now listen to a panel discussion. Check your prediction.**

🎧 **Listen to the audio again and answer the questions. Circle your answers.**

MAIN IDEA

1. What is the main topic?
   A. various Native Alaskan cultures
   B. Native Alaskan languages
   C. education among Native Alaskans
   D. foods among Native Alaskan groups

DETAIL

2. Where do the Inupiaq live?
   A. the Aleutian Islands
   B. the interior part of Alaska
   C. northern Alaska
   D. southern Alaska

3. What do the Inupiaq gather?
   A. fruits and vegetables
   B. seabird eggs
   C. fish
   D. sea mammals

4. Nomadic groups like the Athabascans stay in one place permanently.
   A. True
   B. False

5. Native Alaskans traded food
   A. to share with their community
   B. as a custom
   C. to have more variety
   D. all of the above

6. The Inupiaqs believe spirits move from one life to the next life.
   A. True
   B. False

7. In Athabascan culture who helps raise the children instead of the father?
   A. their mother's father
   B. their mother's brother
   C. their father's father
   D. their father's brother

8. Aleut hats were a symbol of the hunter's skill.
   A. True
   B. False

INFERENCE

9. Which of the following describes Native Alaskan beliefs?
   A. They believe their people walked from Asia to Alaska over the land bridge.
   B. They believe their people came in large boats from the south.
   C. They believe their people were in Alaska from the beginning.
   D. none of the above

10. Why is it difficult for Native Alaskans to keep their traditions?
    A. Traditions are passed down only by the mother's family.
    B. People can no longer hunt or fish in Alaska.
    C. There are many different Native Alaskan languages.
    D. Their traditions don't always fit easily into American culture.

Read this student's journal entry about the panel of Native Alaskans. Notice the bold words. Then match the bold words to their definitions below.

Thursday the 12th

After hearing today's panel I feel very good. I feel like I share ideas about life and the world with the panelists. Many of my **beliefs** are like theirs. The **source** of my beliefs is the natural environment. I believe everything that lives has a **spirit**. I believe the earth, our environment, **connects** the spirits with humans. Our **ancestors** are very important to us in our lives. My ancestors are still with me, every day, even though they no longer live. Last weekend I went fishing and I **caught** a salmon. I felt the spirits of my ancestors who always fished for salmon. They helped me catch my fish last weekend. I **respect** my ancestors, my elders, and culture. I keep my family's **customs**, especially at holiday times, even when I am away from home. My whole life, I have always celebrated holidays **traditionally**, and I always will. It is difficult for me sometimes to fit into **current** popular culture with people my age. In all of these ways I feel very much like the Native Alaskans I saw today. It makes me happy to feel a connection with the native people in Alaska.

A.

1. ancestors ___
2. beliefs ___
3. caught ___
4. connects ___
5. current ___

a. people in one's family who lived a long time ago
b. captured something that you have been chasing or looking for
c. ideas that someone has about religion, politics, etc.
d. of the present time; happening now
e. joins or links to something

B.

1. customs ___
2. respect ___

3. source ___
4. spirit ___

5. traditionally ___

a. admire or honor someone or something
b. a way of behaving which a particular group has had for a long time; traditions
c. a place, person, or thing where something comes or starts from
d. the part of a person that many people believe still exists after the body is dead
e. related to doing things following beliefs from past times

DISCUSS THE THEME

Read these questions and discuss them with a partner. Share your ideas with the class.

1. What are some of your family's traditional customs?

2. Do you feel you belong to current popular culture? Or your traditional culture? Or do you represent both? Explain why.

VOCABULARY REVIEW

WORDS IN CONTEXT

Fill in the blanks with words from each box.

current	land	spirit	wild

1. Many people think the inner _____ continues living after death.
2. Some people think it is difficult to combine _____ culture and traditional beliefs.
3. To many people, it is important to protect _____ plants and animals.
4. Many people also believe in protecting the _____ that is open space outside of cities.

difficulties	environment	searched	transport

5. Explorers to Alaska faced _____ during the harsh winters.
6. Ship captains _____ for safe harbors for their ships.
7. Timber companies _____ wood from the mountain forests to the coast.
8. Native Alaskans have great respect for the _____.

WRONG WORD

One item in each group does not fit. Circle the word.

1. fished   hunted   settled   caught
2. connected   current   present-day   modern
3. family   population   relatives   ancestors
4. miner   ecologist   geologist   member
5. customs   services   legends   traditions
6. discover   search   respect   explore

Fill in the blanks with words from each box.

diversity (*noun*)	diverse (*adjective*)	diversify (*verb*)

1. Languages spoken by Native Alaskans are _____.
2. Cultural _____ makes our society rich and colorful.
3. When businesses increase their types of products, we say they are trying to _____.

economy (*noun*)	economical (*adjective*)	economize (*verb*)

4. People in private business are more successful when the _____ is strong.
5. To save money, it is important to _____.
6. Purchases are _____ if they do not cost too much money.

WRAP IT UP

PROJECT WORK

Survey four people outside of class. Find out what they know about Alaska. Ask the following questions:

- Where is Alaska in relation to the rest of the U.S.?
- When did Alaska become a state?
- What is Alaska famous for?
- Have you ever been to Alaska? Describe your experience.

Present your findings to the class. Discuss the results with your classmates.

INTERNET RESEARCH

Go online and find information about Native Alaskans or immigrants in Alaska. Find answers to the following questions:

- What is the name of the group?
- Where did they live in Alaska?
- What did they do for a living in Alaska?
- What was their life like?

Print a photo of the people you researched, if you can. Present your information to the class.

BUSINESS
TRAVEL

Travelers

Answer these questions.

1. Have you ever traveled for business? Describe your trips.

2. What differences are there between travel for business and for pleasure?

3. If you could travel anywhere tomorrow, where would you go?

61

CHAPTER 1
A TELEVISION TRAVEL GUIDE

◄ A television film crew

PREPARE TO LISTEN

Look at the picture above. Discuss these questions.

1. Have you ever watched TV programs about travel?

2. Where else can you learn about good places to travel?

WORD FOCUS 1

Match the words with their definitions.

abroad	currency	exchange rate	host
beekeeper	episode	gem	sites

1. in or to another country or countries _____
2. the system or type of money that a particular country uses _____
3. a person who introduces a TV or radio show and talks to guests _____
4. places where things of interest happened or existed in the past _____
5. one part of a TV or radio show that continues over time _____
6. the value of money from one country compared to another _____
7. a person who owns and takes care of bees _____
8. a jewel or precious stone _____

MAKE A PREDICTION

The host of the show grew up in Europe.

a. True   **b.** False

🎧 **Now listen to a radio program about a travel show. Check your prediction.**

🎧 **Listen to the audio again and answers the questions. Circle your answers.**

MAIN IDEA

1. What is the main topic?
   A. Megan McCormick is a charming TV actress.
   B. Megan McCormick hosts a popular TV travel show.
   C. Megan McCormick goes on vacation with armchair travelers.
   D. Megan McCormick feels that it is best for people to watch TV for travel.

DETAIL

2. After teaching English in Japan, Megan McCormick
   A. decided to teach English in other countries
   B. went to the Dominican Republic on vacation
   C. studied *National Geographic* to learn about the world
   D. decided to travel as much as possible

3. People can see Megan McCormick's show only in the U.S.
   A. True
   B. False

4. Which of these words is in the title of the show?
   A. trekker
   B. trucker
   C. tricker
   D. tracker

5. Which of the following is **not** true?
   A. Megan McCormick travels anywhere for her show, as long as she is very safe.
   B. Megan McCormick travels anywhere for her show, including places in the U.S.
   C. Megan McCormick travels everywhere and describes every place with great interest.
   D. Megan McCormick travels everywhere and wants her TV audience to travel, too.

6. Which of these words would describe Megan McCormick?
   A. adventurous
   B. respectful
   C. enthusiastic
   D. all of the above

7. According to the speaker, what are some viewers of the show called?
   A. couch potatoes
   B. globe walkers
   C. armchair travelers
   D. travel sitters

8. What happens when Megan McCormick exchanges currency in other countries?
   A. She does it quickly and easily.
   B. She asks someone else to do it for her.
   C. She has the TV crew calculate the exchange rate.
   D. She has to do it slowly to get it right.

INFERENCE

9. Why do people like to watch Megan McCormick's show?
   A. They enjoy watching famous Hollywood stars.
   B. There are no other good programs on TV.
   C. They like to learn about other cultures and places.
   D. They like to hear her sing.

10. According to the speaker, Megan ends her shows
    A. after showing a map of her travel route
    B. with a challenge to her TV audience
    C. with a preview of her next show
    D. with warmhearted comments

Read this e-mail from an international student in the U.S. to a former classmate. Notice the bold words. Then match the bold words to their definitions below.

To: Keiko
Subject: a TV show for practicing your English

Hi, Keiko! I hope you're doing well. I miss you since you went home. I just watched a TV show that you would like. In the U.S. it's called "Globe Trekker," but I think in Japan you will find it called "Pilot Guides." It is a travel show about **intriguing** places to visit all around the world. The shows are very trendy and **hip**. They are all about **adventure**. And each show presents a positive **viewpoint**. I always feel a **longing** for optimistic views when I watch TV.

In the show I just watched they traveled to Inner Mongolia. I did not know anything about that area of China before I saw the show. They visited **local** shopkeepers who sell interesting things. They showed a little about Chinese opera. I could see the **charm** of this traditional style of opera. Also, there was an exciting moment when the host of the show rode some very fast horses. I would never ride those horses. It looked too **perilous**! But it was really fun to watch!

So don't **hesitate**—find out when the show is on in Japan. I think you will like the host's **enthusiasm**. Maybe you will be inspired to become a travel guide! Watch one of the shows and write me about how you like it!

A.

1. adventure ___
2. charm ___
3. enthusiasm ___
4. hesitate ___
5. hip ___

   a. the quality of being pleasant or attractive
   b. very fashionable or knowing a lot about current clothing, music, etc.
   c. an experience or event that is very unusual, exciting, or dangerous
   d. a strong feeling of interest or eagerness
   e. pause before you do something, usually because you are uncertain or worried

B.

1. intriguing ___
2. local ___
3. longing ___
4. perilous ___
5. viewpoint ___

   a. dangerous
   b. from a particular place near you
   c. very interesting; fascinating
   d. a way of looking at a situation; an opinion
   e. a strong wish for something

DISCUSS THE THEME

Read these questions and discuss them with a partner.

1. What unusual place(s) have you traveled to? How did you find out about that place?

2. How can you find out if the show "Globe Trekkers" or "Pilot Guides" is on TV in your area?

Crater of Diamonds
State Park,
Arkansas, USA

Looking for
diamonds

PREPARE TO LISTEN

Look at the map and picture above. Discuss these questions.

1. Have you ever been to the state of Arkansas? What do you know about that part of the U.S.?

2. Where do diamonds come from?

WORD FOCUS 1

Match the words with their definitions.

carat	diamonds	plowed field
crater	minerals	volcano

1. natural substances that are dug out of the ground _____
2. the unit of measurement used to describe how heavy gems are _____
3. the hole at the top of a volcano _____
4. precious stones that are very hard, bright, and expensive _____
5. mountain that can explode, shooting out hot liquid rock _____
6. an area of land with soil that was recently turned over _____

MAKE A PREDICTION

People can find brown diamonds in Arkansas.

a. True   **b.** False

🎧 **Now listen to this radio program on travel. Check your prediction.**

🎧 **Listen to the audio again and answers the questions. Circle your answers.**

MAIN IDEA

1. What is the main topic?
   A. Crater of Diamonds State Park is in Arkansas.
   B. Crater of Diamonds State Park was a privately owned mine until 1972.
   C. Crater of Diamonds State Park is a place where people can look for diamonds.
   D. Crater of Diamonds State Park is similar to state parks all over the world.

DETAIL

2. Crater of Diamonds State Park is the only park in the world where the public can look for diamonds.
   A. True
   B. False

3. Which of the following is **not** true?
   A. The diamonds in Crater of Diamonds State Park are rough.
   B. Most of the diamonds in the park are small.
   C. Other valuable stones are found at Crater of Diamonds State Park.
   D. The diamonds in the park are ready to use in a ring.

4. Diamonds exist in this state park because of
   A. the rich soil
   B. a volcano
   C. an accidental mining explosion
   D. all of the above

5. How much does it cost to look for diamonds in the park?
   A. nothing
   B. less than the cost of a movie ticket
   C. about $100 per day
   D. more than $1,000 per week

6. What did John Huddleston do?
   A. He found the first recorded diamond on this land.
   B. He left a great deal of money to charity after he died.
   C. He made Crater of Diamonds into a tourist attraction.
   D. all of the above

7. The largest diamond ever found in North America was 14.33 carats, and its name is "Uncle Sam."
   A. True
   B. False

8. How many people have found gems at Crater of Diamonds since it became a state park in 1972?
   A. around 40
   B. over 25,000
   C. over 100,000
   D. over one million

INFERENCE

9. When is a good time to go to Crater of Diamonds?
   A. when the ground is dry and hard
   B. in winter when it snows
   C. after it rains
   D. when it is windy

10. Why do people ask for official certification?
    A. for proof that what they found is a real gem
    B. because some of the diamonds in the park aren't real
    C. to prove they paid for their diamonds
    D. because they want to be treated like local visitors

Read this excerpt from a biography of John Huddleston. Notice the bold words. Then match the bold words to their definitions below.

In August 1906, John Wesley Huddleston found diamonds in Pike County, Arkansas. He was farming his land when he noticed the sparkle of a stone in the ground. He knew **whatever** he saw was not just an ordinary stone. He got down on the ground on his hands and knees to look closely. He had never seen anything so shiny. He thought the **likelihood** was great that this was an important **discovery**. He was much too excited to **dig** more holes for planting. So he immediately left his farm to go into town to get the stone **certified** by a jeweler. Before he even left his property, he saw another shiny stone on the surface of the ground. It was a second diamond. In the town of Little Rock, Arkansas, Huddleston's stones were **recorded** officially as blue-white diamonds. After that, the **public** called him the "Diamond King." But life was hard in those days, and even the "Diamond King" had some bad luck and **setbacks**. His bad luck did not **involve** his diamond discoveries. In fact, the thrill he felt from those discoveries kept him happy through his hardships. His burial site is near the **tourist attraction** of Crater of Diamonds State Park.

A.
1. certified ___
2. dig ___
3. discovery ___
4. involve ___
5. likelihood ___

a. move earth and make a hole
b. be concerned with something
c. finding something that no one had ever found before
d. probability
e. said that something is true or correct; documented

B.
1. public ___
2. recorded ___
3. setbacks ___
4. tourist attraction ___
5. whatever ___

a. no matter what
b. documented something in writing
c. people in general
d. difficulties or problems that stop you from making progress
e. a place of interest to visitors

DISCUSS THE THEME

Read these questions and discuss them with a partner. Share your ideas with the class.

1. If you discovered a big diamond, would you keep it or sell it? Why?

2. After hearing about Crater of Diamonds State Park, do you want to travel there? Why or why not?

CHAPTER 3
ON THE ROAD

◀ Business travelers at the restaurant in an airport hotel

PREPARE TO LISTEN

Look at the picture above. Discuss these questions.

1. Have you ever traveled on business? Tell about it.

2. Have you ever started a conversation with another traveler? How would you describe yourself to a new person?

WORD FOCUS 1

Match the words with their definitions.

on the road	shy	talkative
outgoing	strangers	

1. friendly and interested in other people and new experiences _____
2. tending to speak a lot _____
3. nervous and uncomfortable with other people _____
4. traveling (*informal*) _____
5. people that you do not know _____

MAKE A PREDICTION

These business travelers both live in Hong Kong.

a. True   **b.** False

🎧 **Now listen to a conversation between two travelers. Check your prediction.**

🎧 **Listen to the audio again and answers the questions. Circle your answers.**

MAIN IDEA

1. What is the main topic?
   A. Traveling changes people.
   B. Talking over dinner is difficult.
   C. Business travelers miss people from home.
   D. Becoming outgoing is a personality change.

DETAIL

2. Both of the speakers travel for business.
   A. True
   B. False

3. What does the speaker mean by "English gives me an edge."
   A. English gives him a headache.
   B. English makes him nervous.
   C. English puts him in a difficult position.
   D. English gives him an advantage.

4. What are the men doing?
   A. talking about their bosses
   B. having a meeting
   C. sharing experiences
   D. none of the above

5. The man from Hong Kong changed because of his traveling. He said he became more
   A. competitive
   B. open to negotiation
   C. tolerant
   D. articulate

6. The man from Mexico and Texas changed because of his traveling. He said he became more
   A. competent
   B. outgoing
   C. alone
   D. adventurous

7. Which word is the opposite of *outgoing*?
   A. friendly
   B. talkative
   C. shy
   D. unfriendly

8. What did the men order for dinner?
   A. vegetable dishes
   B. special combinations
   C. chicken and rice, burger and fries
   D. fish specials

INFERENCE

9. The men are having dinner together because
   A. they are old friends
   B. they work at the same company
   C. they don't want to eat alone
   D. all of the above

10. What is one thing the men probably did?
    A. They gave each other business cards.
    B. They promised to meet again next month.
    C. They asked how much money each one earns.
    D. They offered to visit each other for a vacation.

Read this e-mail to a former English teacher. Notice the bold words. Then match the bold words to their definitions below.

TO: Ms. Hatch

From: Chang-rae Park

Greetings from New York City! It feels like a very long time ago that you were my teacher. Now I work in New York and live in New Jersey. I love it! I want to thank you in a most **sincere** way for being such a patient and **tolerant** teacher. I learned a great deal, and I have quite an **advantage** over others in my field because of your teaching. It was a great **relief** to me when I arrived in New York and **noticed** that my English was pretty good. Before leaving home, I suffered from a **fear** of doing business in English. I think I was nervous about leaving my family and friends. But right away in New York I was able to **negotiate** in my business discussions. People **trust** me. And my English keeps improving. Also my **personality** is more outgoing and optimistic. I was pretty shy when I studied in your class. It's a big change for me. You said once that we could live our dreams. I **agree** with you. And I am living my dream right now. Thank you.

Sincerely, Park

A.

1. advantage ___   **a.** something that may help you do better than other people

2. agree ___   **b.** have the same opinion as someone

3. fear ___   **c.** talk to someone in order to decide or agree on something

4. negotiate ___   **d.** saw and was aware of something

5. noticed ___   **e.** the feeling when something dangerous, painful, or frightening might happen

B.

1. personality ___   **a.** the good feeling when something unpleasant stops or becomes less strong

2. relief ___   **b.** the qualities and features of a person

3. sincere ___   **c.** able or willing to accept something you do not agree with

4. tolerant ___   **d.** believe that someone will do what they say

5. trust ___   **e.** meaning or believing what you say; honest

DISCUSS THE THEME

Read these questions and discuss them with a partner. Share your ideas with the class.

1. Do you think people can really change their personalities? Why or why not?

2. Have you changed because of travel? In what ways?

VOCABULARY REVIEW

WORDS IN CONTEXT

Fill in the blanks with words from each box.

advantage	discovery	enthusiasm	viewpoint

1. The two brothers tend to have the same _____ on life. They have the same beliefs and always agree about everything.

2. Many years ago the boss made a _____ of a lifetime. She has been wealthy ever since.

3. My friend's ability to speak two languages was a big _____ over the other candidates for the job.

4. The crowd felt the speaker's _____. Soon everybody was clapping and cheering.

intriguing	noticed	sincere	trust

5. I am reading a great book right now. It presents a/an _____ new idea about personality.

6. There is a movie in the theaters now that first came out a year ago, but no one _____.

7. We've been friends for many years. I know I can _____ her.

8. The presenter might not have been interesting, but he was certainly _____.

WRONG WORD

One word in each group does not fit. Circle the word.

1. outgoing   on the road   on the go   traveling
2. host   personality   beekeeper   shopkeeper
3. setback   support   advantage   edge
4. chances   possibility   currency   likelihood
5. recorded   certified   hesitated   documented
6. carat   volcano   diamond   gem

WORD FAMILIES

Fill in the blanks with words from each box.

certification (*noun*)	certified (*adjective*)	certify (*verb*)

1. There are times when it is important to _____ that something is real.
2. I had to send a check to the government for taxes, so I got a _____ check from the bank.
3. People applying for jobs have to show _____ of their legal employment status.

tolerance (*noun*)	tolerant (*adjective*)	tolerate (*verb*)

4. The most important personality trait I learned from my parents is _____.
5. My aunt has several strange co-workers, but she can _____ them all.
6. My boss is not very _____ about casual clothing in the office.

WRAP IT UP

PROJECT WORK

Survey 2–4 people outside of class about a recent trip. Ask them the following questions:

- Was the trip for business, or was it a vacation?
- Where did they go, and how did they decide to go to that place?
- Did they do something on the trip that was fun or unusual?
- Do they recommend the place to others to visit?

Present your findings to the class. Discuss the results with your classmates.

INTERNET RESEARCH

Go online and find information about Crater of Diamonds State Park. Find answers to the following questions:

- How big (how many carats) was the most recent diamond found at the park?
- How many miles would you have to drive a rental car from an airport to visit the park? (You decide which airport.)
- What cities are close by? How much does it cost to camp at the park? Where can you stay near the park?

Print a picture, if you can. Present your information to the class.

HISTORY
MEXICO

"De la Conquista a 1930" ("From the Conquest
to 1930") by Diego Rivera, 1886–1957

BEFORE YOU LISTEN

Answer these questions.

1. Mexican artists are well known for their murals. What is a mural?

2. Describe the mural above.

3. What does this mural tell you about Mexican history?

CHAPTER 1
THE AZTECS

An Aztec drawing of a ball game

PREPARE TO LISTEN

Look at the picture above. Discuss these questions.

1. What does the picture show about Aztec culture?
2. How do you think this game was played?

WORD FOCUS 1

Match the words with their definitions.

harvests	palaces	religion	temples
life expectancy	pyramid	sacrifice	

1. large stone structures with square bases and walls with three sides _____
2. buildings where people pray and worship in some religions _____
3. very large houses where kings and queens live _____
4. the cutting and picking of crops when they are ready _____
5. the offering of an animal or person that has been killed to a god _____
6. the belief in a god or gods who made the world and who can control what happens in it _____
7. the number of years that a person is likely to live _____

MAKE A PREDICTION

The Aztecs ate similar foods to Mexicans of today.

a. True   **b.** False

🎧 **Now listen to a discussion about the Aztecs. Check your prediction.**

🎧 **Listen to the audio again and answer the questions. Circle your answers.**

MAIN IDEA

1. What is the main topic?
   A. The Aztecs built a large city in central Mexico.
   B. Three students discuss their oral presentation project.
   C. The Aztecs tried to please the gods through human sacrifice.
   D. Three students prepare a presentation on aspects of Aztec life.

DETAIL

2. Which three topics did the students decide to focus on?
   A. religion, food, and recreation
   B. religion, language, and education
   C. religion, government, and the arts
   D. religion, education, and architecture

3. Which part of the presentation do the students discuss first?
   A. the architecture of the Aztecs
   B. the location of a large Aztec city
   C. a general introduction about the Aztecs
   D. types of recreation enjoyed by the Aztecs

4. The Aztec city of Tenochtitlán
   A. was destroyed before the Spanish arrived
   B. had a population of about 20,000 people
   C. was built from the 4th to the 6th centuries
   D. had many public and religious buildings in its center

5. Why did one student, Linda, choose food as her topic?
   A. She likes to eat Mexican food.
   B. She is majoring in agriculture.
   C. She is not interested in religion.
   D. She couldn't find information about anything else.

6. The victims of human sacrifice were considered to be
   A. food for the gods
   B. friends of the Spanish
   C. enemies of the Aztecs
   D. messengers to the Aztec gods

7. What was the life expectancy of the Aztecs?
   A. under 40 years
   B. about 50 years
   C. about 60 years
   D. about 70 years

8. What did the student know about the Aztec game?
   A. The players used a stone ball.
   B. The players didn't use their hands.
   C. The players kicked the ball to a net.
   D. There were two teams of 11 players.

INFERENCE

9. Which of the following is true?
   A. The Aztecs considered their gods kind and loving.
   B. The kings and queens were messengers to the gods.
   C. The general population didn't eat enough nutritious food.
   D. Most Aztecs ate a lot of meat in their diet.

10. Why was religion the first topic discussed by the students?
    A. Jason hadn't done his research.
    B. Michael had done his research well.
    C. Religion was the most interesting topic.
    D. All parts of Aztec life depended on religion.

Read this e-mail outline of a presentation. Notice the bold words. Then match the bold words to their definitions below.

Here is an outline of our oral **presentation**. We still need to add details in some places.

The Aztecs

I. Introduction
   a. Aztecs lived in central Mexico from the 14th to 16th centuries
   b. Capital was Tenochtitlán, population 200,000. City was built on islands in a shallow lake. It had palaces, temples, a large pyramid, and other public buildings.
   c. Spanish **destroyed** the city in 1521

II. Religion
   a. Aztec religion focused on having good harvests and pleasing the gods
   b. **Victims** of sacrifice were **captives** from wars and were **considered** messengers to the gods

III. Food
   a. Main form of **agriculture** was growing vegetables. They ate a **vegetarian** diet of corn, beans, squash, tomatoes, and peppers.
   b. Also ate **insects** (which have a higher protein content than meat)
   c. Drank chocolate and a drink called pulque
   d. Life expectancy for Aztecs was only 37 years, partly because of **malnutrition**

IV. Recreation
   a. Played a kind of basketball with a rubber ball and a stone ring

V. Conclusion

A.
1. agriculture ___   **a.** thought to be; treated as
2. captives ___   **b.** prisoners
3. considered ___   **c.** the practice of keeping animals and growing crops for food
4. destroyed ___   **d.** small animals, such as bees, flies, and ants, that have six legs
5. insects ___   **e.** damaged something so badly that it can no longer be used

B.
1. malnutrition ___   **a.** people or animals that are injured, killed, or hurt
2. presentation ___   **b.** the activities that you enjoy when you are not working
3. recreation ___   **c.** a person who does not eat meat or fish
4. vegetarian ___   **d.** a talk that gives information on a specific subject
5. victims ___   **e.** bad health because of a lack of food

DISCUSS THE THEME

Read these questions and discuss them with a partner.

1. How were the Spanish able to capture Tenochtitlán so easily?

2. Why do you think the Spanish destroyed the city?

CHAPTER 2
MEXICO CITY

Images of
Mexico City

PREPARE TO LISTEN

Look at the pictures above. Discuss these questions.

1. What can tourists see and do in Mexico City?

2. What might be some advantages of living in Mexico City? What might be some disadvantages?

WORD FOCUS 1

Match the words with their definitions.

cathedral	indigenous	plaza
crafts	murals	

1. large pictures which are painted on walls _____
2. traditional items made by hand with skill _____
3. a large and important church _____
4. describing the original people native to a country _____
5. an open space in a town or city, with buildings around it _____

MAKE A PREDICTION

Mexico City does not have large parks or open spaces.

a. True   **b.** False

🎧 **Now listen to a tour guide talking about Mexico City. Check your prediction.**

🎧 **Listen to the audio again and answer the questions. Circle your answers.**

MAIN IDEA

1. What is the main topic?
   A. The tourists will spend the afternoon in a large city park.
   B. The tour will include the history, art, and recreation of Mexico City.
   C. The tour will visit the Zócalo, the historic center of Mexico City.
   D. The tour guide will take the tour to the best museum in Mexico.

DETAIL

2. The Aztec city of Tenochtitlán provided the stones for
   A. indigenous houses
   B. the Metropolitan Cathedral
   C. the house of the Mexican president
   D. the National Museum of Anthropology

3. Which building is **not** part of the Zócalo?
   A. the National Palace
   B. the government building
   C. the Metropolitan Cathedral
   D. the National Museum of Anthropology

4. What does the tour guide recommend about buying crafts?
   A. The tourists should not forget to pay.
   B. The tourists should buy crafts in stores.
   C. The tourists should pay in Mexican pesos.
   D. The tourists should bargain for a good price.

5. What is inside the National Palace?
   A. people selling Mexican crafts
   B. murals painted by Diego Rivera
   C. clothes made by indigenous people
   D. beautiful decorations and religious paintings

6. How much does it cost to go up the tower in the Metropolitan Cathedral?
   A. nothing
   B. 10 pesos
   C. 10 dollars
   D. 100 pesos

7. Which of the following is **not** in the Hall of Indigenous Cultures?
   A. historic murals
   B. cultural objects
   C. religious objects
   D. traditional clothes

8. What activities can people do in Chapultepec Park?
   A. go to the zoo
   B. visit museums
   C. buy sidewalk crafts
   D. all of the above

INFERENCE

9. Which is probably the best way to get around Mexico City?
   A. by bus
   B. by car
   C. by subway
   D. by bicycle

10. Mexico City is a good place for tourists to visit because
   A. they can get around Mexico City easily on foot
   B. they can bargain for crafts with sidewalk sellers
   C. they can visit a variety of historical and cultural attractions
   D. they can participate in political demonstrations in the Zócalo

WORD FOCUS 2

Read this postcard that a woman on the tour sent to her friend. Notice the bold words. Then match the bold words to their definitions below.

Hi Angela!

I had a great day seeing the **sights** in Mexico City today. First we went to the Zócalo in the center. It's **surrounded** by some of the city's most important buildings which are built with stones from the Aztec **ruins**. We saw a **demonstration** going on in the plaza—it was quite exciting! I also bought a ring from an indigenous woman, but I found that it's really hard to **bargain**! Next we went to see the wonderful murals by Diego Rivera in the **courtyard** of the National Palace. The last place we visited in the Zócalo was the Metropolitan Cathedral. It's full of beautiful **decorations** and religious art. I was very impressed! Later we went to the National Museum of Anthropology and Chapultepec Park. We had to **head for** the hotel at 3:00 because the **rush hour traffic** in Mexico City is really terrible! Tomorrow we head for home. See you soon!

Janet

A.

1. bargain ___
2. courtyard ___
3. decorations ___
4. demonstration ___
5. head for ___

a. a public protest or march
b. try to persuade someone to lower a price
c. things that are added in order to make something else look more attractive
d. move toward a place
e. an open area without a roof in the center of a house or building

B.

1. ruins ___
2. rush hour ___
3. sights ___
4. surrounded ___
5. traffic ___

a. all the vehicles that are on the road
b. what is left after something is destroyed
c. places of interest that are often visited by tourists
d. the time each day when traffic is busiest because people are traveling to or from work
e. went all around someone or something

DISCUSS THE THEME

Read these questions and discuss them with a partner.

1. Which of the three places visited on the tour would you most like to visit? Why?

2. What would you do in a two-day visit to Mexico City? What other places could you visit, and what other things could you do?

CHAPTER 3
MEXICAN PYRAMIDS

The Pyramid of the Sun,
Teotihuacán, Mexico

PREPARE TO LISTEN

Look at the picture above. Discuss these questions.

1. How does this pyramid look different from an Egyptian pyramid?
2. What was the purpose of Mexican pyramids?

WORD FOCUS 1

Match the words with their definitions.

bury	hidden	steps
calendar	shadows	

1. located where it cannot be seen _____
2. surfaces on which you put your foot when you are going up or down stairs, a ladder, etc. _____
3. put a dead body in a final resting place or grave _____
4. a system for dividing time into fixed periods and for marking the beginning and ending of the year _____
5. dark shapes on a surface caused by something between the light and that surface _____

MAKE A PREDICTION

Egypt has more pyramids than Mexico does.

a. True   **b.** False

🎧 **Now listen to a lecture about the Mexican pyramids. Check your prediction.**

🎧 **Listen to the audio again and answer the questions. Circle your answers.**

MAIN IDEA

1. What is the main topic?
   A. Mexican pyramids were for religious, cultural, and administrative purposes.
   B. Mexican pyramids are different from Egyptian pyramids.
   C. A lot can be learned about early Mexicans by examining their many pyramids.
   D. The largest pyramid in the world is in Mexico.

DETAIL

2. What was the topic of the previous lecture?
   A. Egyptian pyramids
   B. Mexican pyramids
   C. European cathedrals
   D. European buildings

3. Which statement does **not** describe Egyptian pyramids?
   A. They were built in the desert.
   B. They are pointed at the top.
   C. They have steps up the sides.
   D. They have royal leaders buried inside them.

4. Which statement does **not** describe Mexican pyramids?
   A. They are pointed at the top.
   B. They have steps up the sides.
   C. They were used for religious purposes.
   D. They were built in the middle of cities.

5. The Pyramid of the Sun
   A. has 248 steps
   B. was painted yellow
   C. was built in 15 A.D.
   D. is the largest pyramid in the world

6. The largest pyramid at Palenque is the
   A. Pyramid of the Sun
   B. Pyramid of Kukulcán
   C. Pyramid of the Mayans
   D. Temple of the Inscriptions

7. The Pyramid of Kukulcán is unusual because
   A. it is in the shape of a snake
   B. it was painted red
   C. it is a stone calendar
   D. it is in a beach resort

8. Cancun is
   A. a beach resort
   B. near a Mayan pyramid
   C. in southeastern Mexico
   D. all of the above

INFERENCE

9. People who take their vacations on the beaches of Cancun might take a day trip to
   A. Palenque
   B. Teotihuacán
   C. Mexico City
   D. Chichen Itza

10. What is probably true about the importance of Mexican pyramids in the past?
    A. They were only used for burials.
    B. They were only used by royal leaders.
    C. They were only used for special events.
    D. They were the center of religious and cultural life.

Read this summary that a student wrote in a test about the differences between Egyptian and Mexican pyramids. Notice the bold words. Then match the bold words to their definitions below.

Egyptian pyramids are better known than Mexican pyramids, but there are actually more pyramid **structures** in Mexico than in Egypt. Mexico also has the world's largest pyramid, hidden under grass and trees. The pyramids in each country look different and were built for different purposes.

Egyptian pyramids were built to bury **royal** leaders. They were built in the **desert** a long way from cities. They have three **smooth** sides and a **pointed** top. The royal burials are in the **interior** of the pyramids.

Mexican pyramids were built during different time **periods** when new leaders came to **power** and then disappeared. They were built for administrative, religious, and cultural activities. They were built in the center of cities. There are steps up the sides leading to a temple at the top. The temple was used for religious purposes, including human sacrifice.

Some temples have unusual features. The Pyramid of the Sun at Teotihuacán was painted bright red and looked like fire at **sunset**. The Pyramid of Kukulcán at Chichen Itza, near the beach **resort** of Cancun, was designed as a calendar. The shape of a snake can also be seen in the shadows on the stairs.

A.

1. desert ___
2. interior ___
3. periods ___
4. pointed ___
5. power ___

a. having a point at one end
b. a large area of land, usually covered with sand, that has very little water and very few plants
c. on the inside
d. control or influence over other people
e. lengths of time in history

B.

1. resort ___
2. royal ___
3. smooth ___
4. structures ___
5. sunset ___

a. connected with a king, queen, or a member of his or her family
b. buildings or things made from a number of parts
c. the time when the sun goes down and night begins
d. a place where people can stay on vacation and do activities such as swimming and golf
e. having a flat surface with no rough areas

DISCUSS THE THEME

Read these questions and discuss them with a partner.

1. Mexican pyramids were important for government, religion, and cultural activities. What kinds of activities probably took place there regularly?

2. The three Mexican pyramids described in the lecture are located in different areas of Mexico. Which one would you prefer to visit? Why?

VOCABULARY REVIEW

Fill in the blanks with words from each box.

malnutrition	structures	vegetarians	victims

1. The Aztecs were mainly _____, but they also ate insects in their diet.

2. The life expectancy of Aztecs was only 37 years, partly because of _____ caused by a poor diet.

3. The Aztecs considered the _____ of human sacrifice to be messengers to the gods.

4. The Spanish destroyed many of the Aztecs' public _____ in 1521.

courtyard	decorations	sights	traffic

5. The rush hour _____ in Mexico City is so bad that most tourists take the metro or subway.

6. The cathedral in Mexico City contains beautiful _____ and religious paintings.

7. There are many interesting _____ in Mexico City, including museums, parks, and historic buildings.

8. The walls in the _____ of the National Palace are covered with murals painted by Diego Rivera.

WRONG WORD

One word in each group does not fit. Circle the word.

1. inside	interior	insect	inner
2. building	pyramid	structure	recreation
3. destroyed	ruined	damaged	bargained
4. periods	prisoners	victims	captives
5. believed	thought	headed	considered
6. power	control	strength	desert

WORD FAMILIES

Fill in the blanks from each box.

> decorations (*noun*)   decorative (*adjective*)   decorate (*verb*)

1. For special religious events, Mexicans _____ the churches with flowers.
2. Tourists who come to Mexico are fascinated by the beautiful _____ in the public buildings.
3. Many _____ items are sold by sidewalk artists in Mexico City.

> demonstration (*noun*)   demonstrator (*noun*)   demonstrate (*verb*)

4. The many old structures in Mexico _____ the history and culture of the country.
5. Several hundred people were expressing their political opinions during a _____ in the Zócalo.
6. One _____ was arrested by the police.

WRAP IT UP

PROJECT WORK

Survey two people outside of class. Ask them questions about their knowledge of Mexico. Add two or three questions of your own.

- Where and when did the Aztecs live in Mexico?
- What are some of the famous sites in Mexico City?
- Why is Diego Rivera famous?
- What does a Mexican pyramid look like?

Present your findings to the class. Discuss the results with your classmates.

INTERNET RESEARCH

With a partner, go online and find information about tourist sights in Mexico City. Plan a two-day trip to Mexico City with your partner, including the following:

- hotel and transportation around Mexico City
- meals and shopping
- museums, churches, parks, historic buildings

Print photos, if you can. Present your information to the class.

TECHNOLOGY
TRANSPORTATION

A car of the future

BEFORE YOU LISTEN

Answer these questions.

1. What have you used to travel from one place to another? Think of all types of transportation—don't forget your feet.

2. Humans have created many things to make traveling easier. Name as many as possible. Explain how they help humans travel.

3. What are some new ideas in transportation?

A flying car invented by Carl Dietrich of Terrafugia, Inc.

PREPARE TO LISTEN

Look at the picture above. Discuss these questions.

1. Describe the vehicle in the picture.
2. How would a flying car be useful?

WORD FOCUS 1

Match the words with their definitions.

aeronautics	GPS navigation system	landing	propeller
aerospace engineer	hybrid automobiles	license	

1. coming down to the ground in an airplane _____
2. a person whose job it is to design and build airplanes _____
3. the science of aircraft and flight (takes a singular verb) _____
4. a piece of equipment with several blades, which turns very fast in order to make an aircraft move _____
5. cars that use more than one source of power, often gas and electricity _____
6. a satellite system for finding locations _____
7. an official document showing you are allowed to do or have something _____

MAKE A PREDICTION

Carl Dietrich, inventor of the flying car, is a famous astronaut from the 1970s.

a. True   **b.** False

🎧 **Now listen to a radio program. Check your prediction.**

🎧 **Listen to the audio again and answer the questions. Circle your answers.**

MAIN IDEA

1. What is the main topic?
   A. Many people have tried to invent a car that flies.
   B. Carl Dietrich's flying car will have a GPS navigation system.
   C. Terrafugia is going to manufacture the most current travel technology.
   D. Carl Dietrich and his company are inventing a car that flies.

DETAIL

2. According to the passage, the wheel was invented for carrying things and for traveling more easily.
   A. True
   B. False

3. What is **not** an example of recent technology for travel?
   A. cars with GPS navigation systems
   B. hybrid cars
   C. high-speed trains
   D. model airplanes

4. What is the academic field that Carl Dietrich works in?
   A. economics
   B. undersea biology
   C. aeronautics
   D. computer engineering

5. Carl Dietrich's flying car will use gasoline.
   A. True
   B. False

6. Which of the following is true?
   A. Other flying cars didn't work very well, or they were too expensive.
   B. Henry Ford lost a friend in an accident with a flying car model.
   C. People have been working on flying cars for almost 100 years.
   D. all of the above

7. What did Carl Dietrich decide to name his flying car?
   A. Escape from Land
   B. Terrafugia
   C. Transition
   D. Aerocar

8. Henry Ford believed flying cars would be invented.
   A. True
   B. False

INFERENCE

9. Why does Martinez-Sanchez compare Dietrich to Thomas Edison?
   A. to show what a great inventor Dietrich is
   B. because Dietrich borrowed ideas from Edison
   C. to show that both were working on flying cars
   D. because both loved to fly airplanes

10. After Dietrich completes the invention of this flying car, he will probably
    A. invest the money and retire early
    B. change his career to become an undersea biologist
    C. invent something else because he loves to invent things
    D. teach at a university, which has been his dream since he was a child

Read this letter from a college student to his uncle. Notice the bold words. Then match the bold words to their definitions below.

Dear Uncle,

I hope you are well. I'm happy to tell you I just bought a car—a hybrid car! I've been waiting for a long time to own a **vehicle**. After you told me about hybrid automobiles, I was **curious**, so I did some research. I learned how much cleaner the environment could be if people used less gasoline. The **advancements** in hybrid engineering have been huge in recent years!

I am so glad this **technology** made it to the **mass market**. I understand it costs a lot to **manufacture** hybrid vehicles. Still, I hope the day comes soon when hybrids cost less so that more people can afford to buy them. There must be a way to **produce** hybrids at a good price.

Maybe my friends and I can create a start-up company to manufacture hybrid cars or, if not the cars, maybe parts for hybrid engines. When we were kids in school together one of my friends **invented** a part that is now in many vacuum cleaners. That would be great! The three of us could be **colleagues** running a company together manufacturing parts for the hybrid automobile industry!

Well, Uncle, thank you for telling me about hybrid cars. Not only do I have a new car, but maybe I will **transform** myself into a businessman in the next couple of years! Very exciting!

All the best to you,
Kim

A.
1. advancements ___
2. colleagues ___
3. curious ___
4. invented ___
5. manufacture ___

a. eager to know or learn as much as you can
b. people that you work with in a job, especially in a profession
c. make something in large quantities using machines
d. thought of or made something for the first time
e. progress in some areas

B.
1. mass market ___
2. produce ___
3. technology ___
4. transform ___
5. vehicle ___

a. change something completely
b. a very broad range of people who might want to buy something
c. make (or sometimes grow) something
d. the use of science for practical purposes in industry, etc.
e. something that moves people or things from place to place, especially on land

DISCUSS THE THEME

Read these questions and discuss them with a partner.

1. If you could start a new company, what would you like your company to do (or produce)?

2. What academic subjects do you think inventors should study? Explain why.

CHAPTER 2
THE WORLD'S FASTEST SUBWAY

The regular subway, the metro, in Guangzhou, China

PREPARE TO LISTEN

Look at the picture above. Discuss these questions.

1. In what cities have you ridden subways, or metros? Which subway was best? Why?

2. What is your favorite way to travel in a big city? Explain why.

WORD FOCUS 1

Match the words with their definitions.

Canton	glacier	Silk Road	subway
export commodities	seaport	sister cities	

1. a town with a harbor for large ships _____
2. products sold outside the country where they come from _____
3. very old trade routes from China to Europe _____
4. what Guangzhou was called in the past _____
5. towns or cities in different countries that have a special relationship _____
6. a huge mass of ice that moves slowly across land _____
7. underground train system in a city _____

MAKE A PREDICTION

Guangzhou, China, has a subtropical climate.

a. True   **b.** False

🎧 **Now listen to a radio broadcast. Check your prediction.**

🎧 **Listen to the audio again and answer the questions. Circle your answers.**

MAIN IDEA

1. What is the main topic?
   - **A.** The fastest subway in the world is in the Chinese city of Guangzhou.
   - **B.** The subway in Guangzhou, China, connects the sprawling city.
   - **C.** Guangzhou is one of the biggest cities in China, so public transportation is important.
   - **D.** Commuters in Guangzhou, China, need more subways to make their daily commute reasonable.

DETAIL

2. What is **not** an example of traveling for adventure?
   - **A.** going up a mountain by foot
   - **B.** sailing down the longest river
   - **C.** going shopping in Paris
   - **D.** taking a boat to an Arctic glacier

3. The fast subway in Guangzhou travels almost three times faster than most other subways.
   - **A.** True
   - **B.** False

4. The length of the high-speed subway line is 84 miles across the city.
   - **A.** True
   - **B.** False

5. How large is the city of Guangzhou?
   - **A.** the largest in China
   - **B.** the third largest in China
   - **C.** the fifth largest in China
   - **D.** the tenth largest in China

6. What happens at the Canton Fair?
   - **A.** International business people attend.
   - **B.** People see new exports.
   - **C.** Business people discuss their work.
   - **D.** all of the above

7. What is Guangzhou called?
   - **A.** the City of Festivals
   - **B.** the Flower City
   - **C.** the Dragon City
   - **D.** the May City

8. Which of the these countries has one of Guangzhou's sister cities?
   - **A.** Peru
   - **B.** Spain
   - **C.** Poland
   - **D.** Thailand

INFERENCE

9. What is probably true about the subways and the Asian Games in 2010?
   - **A.** At least some of the new subways will be high-speed subways.
   - **B.** Commuters in Guangzhou will have to wait until after 2010 for more subways.
   - **C.** Commuting will be even more inconvenient with more subway lines.
   - **D.** all of the above

10. Why has Guangzhou always been a center of business in China?
    - **A.** The roads are made of silk.
    - **B.** It is in a very good location.
    - **C.** The people like sports.
    - **D.** European traders liked the cuisine.

Read this e-mail to a colleague working on a project in China. Notice the bold words. Then match the bold words to their definitions below.

Greetings! I hope you're enjoying your project and your stay in China.

I'll be attending the Canton Fair this spring. I'd like to spend a few extra days in Guangzhou as a tourist. It's such an important Asian city for **trade** and **commerce**.

I would like to stay downtown where there's some nightlife. I've heard of the local **cuisine**, and can't wait to try out some restaurants in the **urban** center. I also look forward to the mild spring weather. Where I live we're expecting **record-breaking** cold, even into spring.

I'm hoping it might be possible to stay at a hotel downtown near the subway **line** with the high-speed subway train. Even if there are a lot of **commuters**, I want to ride that subway. Public transportation where I live needs so much improvement. Experiencing the other **extreme**—a ride on Guangzhou's new subway, the fastest in the world—will be terrific!

Last night I was talking to a Chinese colleague on the phone about where to stay in Guangzhou. He told me I **mispronounced** all the Chinese words I tried to say. So I will try to improve my accent when I visit next spring.

It will be a **thrill** to visit Guangzhou. Hoping to be able to see you there. Let me know your plans.

Looking forward to hearing from you.

A.

1. commerce ___
2. commuters ___
3. cuisine ___
4. extreme ___
5. line ___

a. people who travel from home to work every day
b. the very best or the very worst of something
c. the activities involved in the business of buying and selling things
d. a style of cooking
e. the route of a subway or railroad

B.

1. mispronounced ___
2. record-breaking ___
3. thrill ___
4. trade ___
5. urban ___

a. describing the best, fastest, highest, coldest, etc.
b. describing a large city
c. a sudden strong feeling of pleasure or excitement
d. buying or selling of things, goods, or services
e. incorrectly said the sounds of a word or part of a word

DISCUSS THE THEME

Read these questions and discuss them with a partner. Share your ideas with the class.

1. Have you ever traveled on some vehicle that is the world's fastest? Or to a place that is the world's highest or lowest? Tell about your experience.

2. Describe a city that you enjoy. What should a traveler visit there? What is the nightlife like?

CHAPTER 3
GLOBAL POSITIONING SYSTEM (GPS)

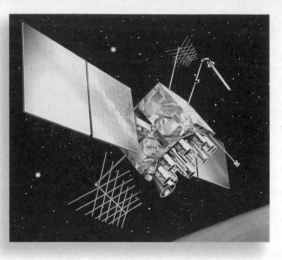

◀ A GPS satellite in orbit

PREPARE TO LISTEN

Look at the picture above. Discuss these questions.

1. What does the GPS satellite in the picture do?

2. How many things do you own that have GPS technology? What are they, and what do they do?

WORD FOCUS 1

Match the words with their definitions.

alert	out of range	tower
hiking	radio waves	

1. invisible sound energy that moves like ocean waves _____
2. a tall narrow building or part of a building _____
3. going for a long walk in the mountains or in the country _____
4. outside the area that something covers _____
5. a warning or possible danger _____

MAKE A PREDICTION

GPS satellites orbit the world.

a. True   **b.** False

🎧 **Now listen to a conversation between two teenage girls. Check your prediction.**

🎧 **Listen to the audio again and answer the questions. Circle your answers.**

MAIN IDEA

1. What is the main topic?
   A. GPS satellites are in orbit around the Earth.
   B. GPS is taking away our privacy.
   C. GPS phones can give directions to various places.
   D. GPS phones do more than just make phone calls.

DETAIL

2. When can GPS help us with directions?
   A. when we are lost
   B. when we are on a trip to a new place
   C. when we don't remember which way to go
   D. all of the above

3. The speaker mentions *location tracking*. What does *tracking* mean?
   A. following where something has gone
   B. recording separate pieces of audio
   C. sporting events such as races held on a field
   D. losing something or forgetting where it is

4. The phone that belongs to the girl's parents tells them when she leaves home.
   A. True
   B. False

5. What does the speaker mean when she says "Oh, I don't mind"?
   A. I don't think so.
   B. I don't agree.
   C. No problem.
   D. I don't understand.

6. How do GPS phones work?
   A. The phones use radio waves from satellites to figure out locations.
   B. Parents call a central office to find out where their children are.
   C. Radio waves travel over phone lines to the cell phone.
   D. all of the above

7. What can cause problems with GPS?
   A. a rainy day
   B. buildings or other tall things
   C. darkness
   D. all of the above

8. Where can you display the GPS information?
   A. on a website
   B. on a map
   C. on a chart
   D. all of the above

INFERENCE

9. If parents know where their child's GPS phone is, they assume
   A. their child can call them any time
   B. they can communicate except in bad weather
   C. their child wants more privacy
   D. they know where their child is

10. One girl wants to be alone sometimes. The other girl feels safe when other people know where she is. A GPS phone is best for the second girl.
    A. True
    B. False

Read this student's journal entry. Notice the bold words. Then match the bold words to their definitions below.

In class we've been studying about new technologies. It makes me wonder about what our future will be like. Humans might live on space stations that are **orbiting** the Earth. And then they might fly through space to go to work during the day on a **satellite**. Amazing! The human population will be larger. That **bothers** me because it will be hard for anyone to find time and place for quiet **privacy**. But there will be good things, like new inventions. I hope someone will invent something that **calculates** nutrients, calories, and fat in meals I want to prepare. Another great thing would be technology to tell us the **exact** time it will take to do something. I really need something like that to help keep me from being late. I don't have any problem with **location** and figuring out which **turn** to make in my car. But I definitely need help estimating the amount of time I need to get things done. I'm probably not **alone** with that problem. The future will bring many inventions and solutions. Technology will make things very different. But I hope the world will not become **totally** different because it's a wonderful place.

A.
1. alone ___   **a.** a place, position, or site
2. bothers ___   **b.** completely correct; accurate
3. calculates ___   **c.** disturbs or annoys someone
4. exact ___   **d.** without any other person
5. location ___   **e.** finds something out by using mathematics

B.
1. orbiting ___   **a.** moving around a planet in space
2. privacy ___   **b.** completely
3. satellite ___   **c.** a change in direction
4. totally ___   **d.** something sent into space to move around a planet for a particular purpose
5. turn ___   **e.** being alone or away from other people who may disturb you

DISCUSS THE THEME

Read these questions and discuss them with a partner. Share your ideas with the class.

1. In what ways will future advances in technology change how people travel? Use your imagination.

2. Imagine someone promised to give you $5 million dollars for inventing some new technology for travel (or entertainment). What would you invent?

VOCABULARY REVIEW

WORDS IN CONTEXT

Fill in the blanks with words from each box.

commerce	exact	manufacture	technology

1. In the world of _____, change is made by economists rather than scientists.
2. Scientists and engineers make advancements in _____.
3. The work that scientists and engineers do is very _____.
4. To _____ a product requires a complex set of processes.

commuters	line	privacy	urban

5. _____ areas can be crowded, and life there can be hectic.
6. Sometimes people travel on the same subway _____ every day at the same time.
7. Regular _____ might see each other at the same time and the same place every day.
8. Having some _____ from time to time can be difficult in a crowded city.

WRONG WORD

One word in each group does not fit. Circle the word.

1. trade   commerce   commuters   business
2. manufacture   mass market   produce   make
3. alone   curious   private   by yourself
4. invented   created   made   traded
5. transform   satellite   planet   orbit
6. city   urban   record-breaking large community

WORD FAMILIES

Fill in the blanks with words from each box.

advancement (*noun*)	advanced (*adjective*)	advance (*verb*)

1. In order to _____ in a sport, it is necessary to practice a great deal every day.
2. Landing on the moon was a significant _____ in the history of space exploration.
3. People who want to be aerospace engineers take _____ science and math courses.

calculation (*noun*)	calculator (*noun*)	calculate (*verb*)

4. For many people it is difficult to do mathematics without a _____.
5. Figuring out a complex statistical _____ requires great care.
6. The assistant will _____ the cost of the project, but the committee will check his work.

WRAP IT UP

PROJECT WORK

**Survey two people outside of class about transportation technology they use.
Ask them the following questions:**

- What transportation technology do they use every morning or almost every morning?
- Ten years ago, what technology did they use?
- What vehicles have they ridden in? (cars, subways, trains, boats, etc.)
- What new inventions for travel would they like to see in the future?

Present your findings to the class. Discuss the results with your classmates.

INTERNET RESEARCH

**Go online and find information about Carl Dietrich's flying car. Try online at the
website for his company, Terrafugia. Find answers to the following questions:**

- What is the most recent news on the flying car?
- What is the most recent quote from Carl Dietrich? (Look through the press releases.)
- Under FAQ, what general questions are there?
- Are there any jobs available?

**Print a photo of the vehicle, if it is convenient. Present your information to
the class.**

ESSENTIAL LISTENING SKILLS: ANSWER KEY AND EXPLANATIONS

WHAT TO DO BEFORE YOU LISTEN

A.

1. *Possible answer:* A baby has on headphones and has a keyboard.

2. *Possible answer:* The passage will discuss babies and music.

B.

1. *Possible answer:* The passage will be about a connection between music and intelligence.

2. *Possible answer:* The baby is listening to music.

3. Answers will vary.

4. Answers will vary.

> **TIP:** Think about what you know about a topic before you listen. As you listen, compare what you hear to what you already know.

C.

1. Answers will vary.

2. Answers will vary.

> **TIP:** Look ahead for any words you may hear before you listen. Then you will be able to recognize these words in the passage.

D.

False. Researchers did not study babies. They studied older students, including college students.

WHAT TO DO WHILE YOU LISTEN

E.

1. What is the main topic?

   A is incorrect. Early childhood development was the topic in the last class.

   B is incorrect. The topic is not limited to babies.

   C is correct.

   D is incorrect. There was no discussion of the relative value of listening to different types of music.

F.

2. The research took place in

A is correct. The research took place in 1993.

B is incorrect. The research used college students, but we don't know if it took place in a college.

C is incorrect. There is no information about a music class.

D is incorrect. There is no information about a music recording company.

> **TIP: Listen carefully for numbers, especially for dates and for the difference between numbers such as 19 and 90.**

3. The students who listened to Mozart

A is incorrect. The students did not do better on all their tests.

B is correct. The students who listened to Mozart did better on the part of the test that tested spatial reasoning.

C is incorrect. The students had higher scores on one part of the test. We don't know if they were more intelligent than the other students.

D is incorrect. All three answers above must be correct for this to be the correct answer.

4. According to the lecture, which of the following is **not** true?

A is not the correct answer because it is true. The researchers did not say anything about intelligence.

B is correct. The researchers did not find that listening to classical music makes children more intelligent.

C is not the correct answer because it is true. Other researchers have not been able to get the same results.

D is not the correct answer because it is true. The students who listened to Mozart had better scores in spatial reasoning.

> **TIP: Be careful of a word like *not*.**

5. What did people remember about news reports on the research results?

A is incorrect. People did not remember that students got higher scores only in a task related to folding paper.

B is incorrect. People did not remember that the effects of listening to classical music only lasted for 10 minutes.

C is correct. People remembered that students got higher scores on a test after they listened to classical music.

D is incorrect. People did not remember or hear that students may have scored higher because they enjoyed the music and were more alert.

> **TIP: Eliminate any choices that you know are wrong.**

6. Which of these is most likely to increase results on math tests?

A is incorrect. Piano practice is not the only type of music study that may improve results in math.

B is incorrect. Folding paper has no relation to math test results. It is connected to spatial reasoning.

C is incorrect. Researchers have not found a link between classical music and math tests.

D is correct. Researchers have found that studying music may improve results in math problems.

> **TIP: Sometimes you need to listen for details in different sections of the passage.**

7. Parents bought CDs with classical music because

A is incorrect. The governor of the state of Georgia included money in the state budget to give every child born in the state a CD of classical music.

B is correct. Parents believed that they could make their children smarter by playing classical music.

C is incorrect. The passage does not say parents wanted children to play classical music.

D is incorrect.

> **TIP: Read the choices carefully.**

8. The speaker thinks that music education is

A is not correct. The speaker thinks that music education is important.

B is correct. The speaker thinks that music education is a beneficial activity.

C is incorrect. The speaker thinks that music education, along with a variety of other subjects, can benefit children but does not say that it is the only way to increase intelligence.

D is not correct.

G.

9. The entrepreneurs started selling CDs with classical music because they wanted to help children be more intelligent.

A is incorrect. The entrepreneurs saw an opportunity to make money.

B is correct.

10. This lecture is probably part of

A is incorrect. This lecture does not have any information about math, so it is probably not part of a math course.

B is correct. This lecture is probably in a teacher education course. The earlier lecture was on early childhood development, and this lecture is on music and intelligence.

C is incorrect. This is not a lecture from a course in medical school.

D is incorrect. The lecture mentions entrepreneurs, but it is probably not part of a business course.

H.

1. C All they said was that listening to Mozart <u>increased students'</u> **performance** <u>on a test</u> of spatial reasoning.

2. B Well, of course **entrepreneurs** saw this as <u>a big opportunity</u>. They <u>started putting together CDs</u> with classical music, mostly Mozart, and <u>sold them to parents</u>.

3. A So, is there a **link** <u>between music and intelligence</u>? No, at least not according to the current research.

4. Spatial reasoning means <u>being able to figure out where things go and to follow patterns</u>.

5. Some of these researchers attributed the improvement to the "enjoyment effect." That is, <u>the students might have been more alert because they had had a pleasant experience</u>.

6. It got misinterpreted. <u>People didn't hear,</u> "its effect lasted for 10 minutes." <u>They heard,</u> "the students got higher scores on a test."

7. They made a lot of claims such as <u>"This CD is designed to improve your baby's mind."</u>

VOCABULARY INDEX

meadows 29
melodramas 38
member 52
mentioned 7
meteorites 20
migration 28
minerals 65
miners 53
miracle 31
misleading 34
mispronounced 91
mistreating 34
modernized 46
modules 17
monk 41
mountain ranges 53
moves 46
murals 77

N

natural disasters 26
negotiate 70
normal 16
noticed 70

O

obstacles 46
on the road 68
orbit 14
orbiting 94
organization 28
originally 43
out of range 92
outgoing 68
outgrew 43

P

palaces 74
panel 50
parachute 14
participated in 10
perform 41
perilous 64
periods 82
personality 70
photo essay 26
photographers 28
photojournalist 26
pipeline 53
plaza 77
plowed field 65
pointed 82
politician 4
popularity 10
population 52

post-war 40
power 82
presentation 76
privacy 94
professional 34
promoting 43
propeller 86
protests 7
province 44
public 67
published 28
punished 46
purity 43
pyramid 74

Q

qualified 16
quarters 17

R

radio waves 92
raised 4
reactions 28
reality 10
record 7
record-breaking 91
recorded 67
recreation 76
recruited 16
redwood trees 29
regret 19
relationship 31
relief 70
religion 74
renowned 40
represents 43
resort 82
respect 31, 58
reunions 19
rivals 5
rockets 20
romantic 46
round 2
royal 82
ruins 79
run for 4
rush hour 79
rusty 44

S

sacrifice 74
satellite 94
satellites 20
scene 32
score 2

seagull 14
seaport 89
searched 52
selection 16
serious 32
services 53
setbacks 67
settled 52
shadows 80
shelter 56
shots 40
shy 68
sights 79
Silk Road 89
sincere 70
sister cities 89
sites 62
smooth 82
soap opera 44
society 4
solo flight 14
sonic boom 20
source 58
sources 8
spectacular cases 22
spectators 5
spirit 58
sportswriter 5
standing room 5
statehood 53
statistics 10
steps 80
strangers 68
structures 82
struggles 40
styles 43
subject 31
subtitles 44
suburb 43
subway 89
suffering 40
sunset 82
supported 4
surface 22
surrounded 79

T

takes place 10
talkative 68
tear down 7
technology 88
temples 74
terrific 7
territory 55

theme 38
thrill 91
thundering 31
tied 8
tolerant 70
totally 94
tourist attraction 67
tower 92
trade 91
traditionally 58
traffic 79
transform 88
transmission 14
transported 55
trophy 8
trust 70
turn 94

U

upsets 8
urban 91

V

variety 22
vegetarian 76
vehicle 88
versions 46
victims 76
viewpoint 64
volcano 65

W

war-torn 2
waterfalls 29
wave 44
whatever 67
whiskers 56
wild 52
wilderness 29
World Cup 5

COMMON IRREGULAR VERBS

INFINITIVE	SIMPLE PAST	PAST PARTICIPLE	INFINITIVE	SIMPLE PAST	PAST PARTICIPLE
be	was/were	been	let	let	let
become	became	become	light	lit/lighted	lit/lighted
begin	began	begun	lose	lost	lost
blow	blew	blown	make	made	made
break	broke	broken	mean	meant	meant
bring	brought	brought	meet	met	met
build	built	built	pay	paid	paid
buy	bought	bought	put	put	put
catch	caught	caught	read	read	read
choose	chose	chosen	ride	rode	ridden
come	came	come	ring	rang	rung
cost	cost	cost	run	ran	run
cut	cut	cut	say	said	said
do	did	done	see	saw	seen
draw	drew	drawn	sell	sold	sold
drive	drove	driven	send	sent	sent
eat	ate	eaten	set	set	set
fall	fell	fallen	show	showed	shown
feel	felt	felt	sing	sang	sung
find	found	found	sit	sat	sat
fly	flew	flown	sleep	slept	slept
forget	forgot	forgotten	speak	spoke	spoken
freeze	froze	frozen	spend	spent	spent
get	got	gotten	stand	stood	stood
give	gave	given	steal	stole	stolen
go	went	gone/been	swim	swam	swum
grow	grew	grown	take	took	taken
hang	hung	hung	teach	taught	taught
have	had	had	tear	tore	torn
hear	heard	heard	tell	told	told
hold	held	held	think	thought	thought
hurt	hurt	hurt	throw	threw	thrown
keep	kept	kept	understand	understood	understood
know	knew	known	wear	wore	worn
lay	laid	laid	win	won	won
leave	left	left	write	wrote	written